Introducing a
School Dog

of related interest

Animal-assisted Interventions for Individuals with Autism
Merope Pavlides
ISBN 978 1 84310 867 2
eISBN 978 1 84642 795 4

The Neurodiverse Classroom
A Teacher's Guide to Individual Learning Needs and How to Meet Them
Victoria Honeybourne
ISBN 978 1 78592 362 3
eISBN 978 1 78450 703 9

Sensory Stories for Children and Teens
with Special Educational Needs
A Practical Guide
Joanna Grace
ISBN 978 1 84905 484 3
eISBN 978 0 85700 874 9

INTRODUCING A SCHOOL DOG

— Our Adventures with — Doodles the Schnoodle

CHERRYL DRABBLE

Jessica Kingsley *Publishers*
London and Philadelphia

First published in 2019
by Jessica Kingsley Publishers
73 Collier Street
London N1 9BE, UK
and
400 Market Street, Suite 400
Philadelphia, PA 19106, USA

www.jkp.com

Library of Congress Cataloging in Publication Data
A CIP catalog record for this book is available from the Library of Congress

British Library Cataloguing in Publication Data
A CIP catalogue record for this book is available from the British Library

ISBN 978 1 78592 477 4
eISBN 978 1 78450 861 6

Printed and bound in Great Britain

This book is dedicated to my brother Terry who has been fighting cancer throughout my writing of this book. He lives on to see the book in print.

Thank you to Lisa Clark and all the publishing team at Jessica Kingsley for endless support and patience.

Contents

Acronyms

ADHD Attention Deficit Hyperactivity Disorder

ASC Autistic Spectrum Condition

ICT Information Communications Technology

PGCE Postgraduate Certificate in Education

PMLD Profound and Multiple Learning Disabilities

PRU Pupil Referral Unit

SLT Senior Leadership Team

TA Teaching Assistant

UK Key Stages and Equivalent US Grades

UK Key Stage	US grade
Early Years Foundation Stage	Pre-kindergarten
Key Stage 1	Kindergarten and 1st Grade
Key Stage 2	2nd Grade to 5th Grade
Key Stage 3	6th Grade to 8th Grade
Key Stage 4	9th Grade and 10th Grade
Key Stage 5	11th Grade and 12th Grade

INTRODUCTION

This is the story of our school's dog. In the following pages I will take you through how and why we decided to add a dog to our school staff team at Highfurlong Special School in Blackpool. I will talk about the dog's expected remit in school and also discuss the practical issues and finances associated with him. Further chapters will look at how we chose our dog and introduced him to the children, the staff and the parents. Later I will reveal many of the successes that we have witnessed in the short time we have had our dog in school. There have been many unexpected benefits which we couldn't possibly have foreseen and which have been life changing for some of our children. There will also be a chapter showing how our ingenious teachers have included the dog in their lessons in order to show the true value of dogs in schools. Read on and enjoy the account.

Since we introduced our school dog in June 2017 I have been asked the following questions several times. What does he actually do in school? Is it just an excuse to take your dog to school? Where does he go all day? 'Does he just sit in your office all day?' asked one local headteacher.

These are the queries I was facing. At the start of my school's journey I also pondered these questions. A search on the internet showed very few books written on the subject so I decided that writing about our experience would be useful for headteachers, teachers, governors, school staff and parents.

Several months ago I watched with interest as a few of the mainstream schools in our locality began to introduce dogs to their schools. The high school next door to us seemed to start the trend in Blackpool and they have two dogs. I began to read blog posts around the subject. I discovered that they have many uses and I could see how valuable one might be for our children.

We are a small, purpose built special school located in Blackpool, North West England and we are renowned for our forward thinking and our creative ideas. Our cohort of children, aged from 2 to 19 years have various special educational needs including complex medical needs, Autistic Spectrum Condition (ASC), profound and multiple learning disabilities (PMLD), attention deficit hyperactivity disorder (ADHD), learning difficulties and behaviour challenges. There must be many benefits for our children from having a dog in school; I now needed to discover those benefits and also convince our headteacher that we needed a dog. I broached the subject with her and she went off to conduct her own research. We have a thoroughly enlightened headteacher and I was able to report a couple of conversations later that she was keen on the idea.

That was just the beginning of our journey. There was a long way to go in terms of choosing the puppy, finances, risk assessments and introducing them to the children. The headteacher and I met many times as we mapped out the future. We were agreed that the dog would need to be highly trained and be super cuddly and gentle for our cohort of very special children and young people. It was time to set about the business of locating Highfurlong's dog.

— Chapter 1 —

RESEARCHING OUR OPTIONS

Before revealing to the children in school the very exciting news that we were to have a puppy on the premises, I decided that it would be a good idea to have them sell the idea to themselves. I utilised a series of Key Stage 5 Information Communications Technology (ICT) lessons and set the young people a mission to find out the therapeutic benefits of animals.

We discovered that 'pet therapy' is a rapidly growing field and a variety of animals are now used. The theory is that animals can help people cope with physical health problems such as cancer and mental health issues such as anxiety and depression and with conditions such as autism, cerebral palsy or Down's syndrome. For children with ASC animals are known to help them to interact socially as they have in their possession a conversation starter. Their sensory issues may be reduced as they become accustomed to the feel of the animal's fur or skin. At the opposite end of the age scale, older people living with Alzheimer's disease or dementia may find that their uncharacteristic agitation and aggressive behaviours are decreased by the presence of an animal. The very presence of an animal sitting with them is known to have a calming influence on the mind.

Throughout their research our Key Stage 5 students discovered that there is a very strong bond between humans and animals and pet therapy harnesses that bond and capitalises on it. Endorphins are released when animals are petted and this produces a calming effect for the person or child concerned. This helps reduce pain and stress and improves overall well-being. As well as dogs, cats and rabbits, surprisingly, some lesser known animals are used as therapy pets, including birds, spiders, fish, guinea pigs, mice, snakes, hedgehogs, alpacas, rats and pigs. None of our children expressed an interest in cuddling rats or snakes! Varndean School even has seven resident pygmy goats. It tweets as @varndeangoats and the goats are fully included in school life. The children learn to feed the goats and to take care of them and their living quarters; in return the goats teach the children about the great outdoors and their way of life.

So, the students in Key Stage 5 were diligent in their research. They also reminded me that we have a rather unusual pet in Circle Class in our school already. Mrs Short, the teacher, is the proud keeper of Trevor the tortoise. Trevor was introduced last year and has been very popular with the children. Trevor has had visitors from all over the school as some of our children have never seen a tortoise and most have never held one. He goes home at weekends with different staff members and returns to be with the children on Monday mornings. Through Trev the children have learnt that animals need food, warmth and shelter. They have learned the specific types of food that tortoises need and also that he needs plenty of exercise. Class staff have made a sign for the classroom door which alerts all visitors to the fact that he is out of his cage. He is allowed to roam freely around the classroom at certain times of the day. He is possibly the most pampered tortoise ever!

The Key Stage 5 students discovered many therapeutic benefits of using pets. They also discovered that the benefits of owning an animal could be mutual. The animal gains through being loved, petted, cared for and highly trained. The health and well-being of both the therapy animal and the owner, the children in our case, are greatly improved through this relationship.

Thanks to the students we had plenty of information about the various animals that we could introduce to our school. We had an idea of how much care and attention they all needed. We also understood what a huge responsibility it would be to own a pet. After much discussion and analysing of information, the children weren't swayed by any of the other animals. They decided that by far the best and most practical animal for our school, if we were going to have a pet, would be a dog. However, they didn't yet know that we were going to have our own dog!

— Chapter 2 —

OUR DECISION TO GET A DOG

The initial decision had been made to have a dog in school. That was as far as the discussions had gone between the headteacher and myself. We had not discussed the finer details and we had not divulged the exciting secret to anyone else in school with the exception of another member of the senior leadership team (SLT).

Thanks to Key Stage 5 we were now fully acquainted with the therapeutic benefits of certain animals. We had ample information to enable a decision to be made. I now needed to determine the benefits of having an actual puppy in school. I felt this was important in case there were any complaints from children, staff, parents or governors. I needed a vast amount of information in order to dispel any myths or to quash any information that might be untrue. I also needed to determine that a dog was the best choice over all the other possible animals that Key Stage 5 had identified.

There are many benefits to having a puppy in school, and they aren't all educational. For example, children who are scared of animals, dogs in particular, will gain a great deal from being in the presence of one that is well controlled and supervised. Having a puppy in school from it being just a few weeks old will allow a timid child to grow close to the puppy and watch it as it grows and matures. They will see all the fun and mischief associated with a boisterous puppy and be able to watch it from a distance. As the puppy emerges from the very playful stage the child will already be attached to it as they have watched it grow, been close to it and probably stroked the animal as it has been maturing from just a few weeks old. At our school we have been witness to this first hand. We have a 14-year-old girl with learning difficulties and some physical challenges who was absolutely terrified of dogs. Her terror was such that she once ran towards the road to get out of the way of a passing dog. She is now over this fear, partly due to being around our school dog. More will follow about this outstanding success later in the book.

Conversely, some children have no respect for animals and therefore have no fear of them. These are the children who are over friendly with dogs and may tease them and run a high risk of being hurt by one. This scenario is just as dangerous as the one above; both need to be handled carefully. The presence of a dog will teach respect for dogs and puppies and will also teach children not to get too close to those sharp, nibbling teeth!

Being around a friendly, bouncy dog will lift the spirits of anyone who has had a playground accident or is in a grumpy mood. Stroking the fur brings instant calm for the pup and the child. This particular benefit is not to be underestimated as we will see later. On the emotional front the sight of a puppy will lift everyone's mood. They are such a bundle of fun, energy and mischief and can reduce most adults and children to giggles in seconds. Also, dogs are known to improve self-esteem. A dog is so attentive to a person that they begin to feel better about themselves as a result. Children will become involved in caring for and exercising the animal and will begin to have a more positive view of themselves as they see themselves achieving success in this area. This is a very important point as when children believe they are valued they take better care of themselves. One of the greatest things to happen from an emotional perspective is the amount of laughter and fun a puppy brings. Most people agree that a puppy's antics are laughter inducing. Again, only the hard hearted will not be moved by the presence of a puppy.

From a physical perspective a dog will help with pain management. Some of our children are living with rather cruel and debilitating diseases that cause them great pain when they try to walk around or move. Of course they try to be brave at all times but just sometimes that physical pain breaks through and they struggle to keep a smile on their faces. The dog brings a renewed determination and motivation to move and walk, if only to chase after the pup. Senses are also heightened around the dog as the children touch the soft fur and feel his cold, shiny, wet, nose.

One more non-educational benefit from having a dog on the school premises is that there is a sense of collective ownership; the family feeling is increased. Children who don't have a pet at home are encouraged to take an active part in walking the dog, petting it and looking after its general well-being. Children gain a sense of importance and take on a caring role that they might not be able to achieve at home and this aids their personal development. Everyone needs to feel loved and wanted and a puppy loves everyone indiscriminately. Having a furry, four-legged friend also helps children to play more sociably with others. The dog will find that it is at the centre of a game and the children may play amicably with those they wouldn't usually associate with. On a similar theme, the presence of a dog may help to give the school a less clinical feel to it. Modern schools are often quite stark with minimal displays to avoid sensory overload for the children. The puppy will help to reduce the almost sterile nature of some schools.

Moving on to the academic benefits of having a school dog on the premises there are several excellent reasons why a school might consider this. For example they make a superb starting point for a conversation in any lesson. Children will chat about their own pets and discuss them in some detail when they are comparing them to the dog that is in front of them. Some rich language will occur as the children set about the business of discussing their pets and comparing them to the school dog. Literacy lessons may involve stories about their own pets or fictional stories involving dogs. Spellings can be devised from items used for the dog and that will give children an interesting theme to work from. Taking responsibility for yourself and for others is a large part of growing up. Being a part of the school dog's life, caring for it and loving it encourages children to take responsibility for themselves. This is a cornerstone of the personal, social, health and economic education (PSHE) curriculum and is an important and valued aspect of the advantages of the dog. Also, being friends with a dog encourages problem solving. If you are in charge of a dog you cannot give up on a problem; you have to find a way to solve it for the sake of the dog. This is a good skill to develop. Sharing and turn taking are areas in which some children struggle. They may have been used to having things all to themselves and not sharing. With a dog they have to learn to take their turn and share.

The research stage was finally over. I had found out via our older students about the various animals we could choose from. We had information about the benefits of each of the individual animals including some rather unusual ones and how our children might be affected by their presence. We knew the mental health benefits we could expect and also the physical gains for our cohort of special children. We now also knew that there would be social benefits and of course we had some information regarding the educational gains we might expect. Most importantly, I now knew that the children in the research party favoured a dog. I gathered all the information together and set off to discuss it with the headteacher.

The headteacher and I discussed the accumulated information and came to the decision that a dog was the pet for us. It would be easier to transport to school and to train than many of the other animals. We then looked at the benefits for specific cohorts of children. For example, for children on the autism spectrum we found out that a puppy would give emotional support and comfort in the form of cuddles. The sensory feel of the fur would be a calming influence. For children with ADHD the dog would calm them down, lower their stress levels and help prepare them for the therapy or the lesson to come. For children with mental health issues such as depression and stress a dog would significantly reduce their stress levels. Also, for our sensory children stroking the fur and touching and cuddling the dog would be a whole new experience for many of them. It seemed we were finally ready to locate our puppy.

— Chapter 3 —

HOW WE CHOSE OUR PUPPY

From the very beginning I had in my mind a picture of the exact type of puppy that I felt would be best for our school. In terms of size we needed a medium sized dog. A large dog might terrify the children and is also impractical for travelling to work in the car or for going on school trips on the minibus with the children later down the line. I also knew that I wanted our puppy to be black. A jet black puppy would stand out beautifully against any colours surrounding him. Any bright accessories he wore or toys he held in his mouth would stand out beautifully against his black fur. This is important for making educational resources that use photographs where contrast is vital. Contrast is also vital for our children and young people with visual impairment. A black dog would stand out from his surroundings making it easier for the children to see him.

There are a number of things to consider when looking for the ideal puppy. First of all you need to choose your breed. Do you want a puppy that is going to be very tall, very small, has lots of energy or is more lethargic? Think it through carefully. Not only does the puppy have a job to do in school but it also has to fit into your family life. Consider who will take it home in the evening. In our case my headteacher and I discussed this and decided that the dog would be mine and accompany me to school. Therefore he needed to fit in with my home life. Consider if you require a pedigree, a crossbreed or a mongrel. Pedigree pups have the advantage that you will be able to say with relative certainty the size, temperament, coat and behaviour of the dog and also the amount of exercise it will need. The main disadvantage of a pedigree is that there may be a genetic disease lurking somewhere in the pedigree. Pedigree dogs also tend to command very fancy prices often reaching into thousands of pounds!

A crossbreed dog is often known as a 'designer' dog and is where both parents are full pedigrees of different breeds. For example a schnauzer and a poodle produce a schnoodle and a cocker spaniel and a poodle produce a cockapoo. These designer dogs are often healthier as they aren't subject to selective breeding and you can generally predict the type of coat, the energy levels and the size of the animal. Prices may come as a shock as they too command a vast amount of money, often up to a thousand pounds.

Mongrels can be problematic. They may be beautiful and have a wonderful temperament that is perfect for school and for being with children. However, you are unlikely to know the parentage of the dog and therefore cannot reliably predict the traits it may display. The big advantage is of course the cost; these puppies will be considerably cheaper.

Once you have chosen your breed you should look for a responsible owner. I am not an expert in this field but there is a lot of useful advice available from animal welfare organisations.[1] In my own experience, when we visited a couple of places in our area and I could tell the owners didn't have the best interests of the pups at heart. They were kept in cramped conditions and had to fight the others for food and water. Eventually we located a very responsible sounding breeder and travelled sixty miles to Manchester to view the pups.

The breed I had settled on was a schnoodle. A schnoodle is part schnauzer and part poodle. I chose this particular designer pup mainly due to the coat being hypoallergenic. This means that the coat doesn't shed hairs and no one, including the children, will be allergic to the dog. This aspect is important to us as many of our children live with life-limiting illnesses and others have additional medical needs and they do not need to be exposed to allergies resulting from pets introduced by staff. Schnauzers are known for being loyal, protective and have above average intelligence. They are also affectionate which makes them ideal for being around children. Poodles are incredibly obedient and are known for their agility and light movements. They are one of the easiest dogs to train due to their high intelligence levels. They are also highly protective, which makes them a good choice for being with children. Between the two dogs, our puppy would have all the characteristics required to make him a good school dog.

The schnauzer is the mummy of the parental team and she is a black standard schnauzer and is around 47 centimetres tall. The father is a chocolate-coloured

---

1   https://www.dogstrust.org.uk/help-advice/advice-for-owners/
     buying-a-dog/buying-a-dog
     https://www.rspca.org.uk/adviceandwelfare/pets/dogs/puppy/
     breeder/-/articleName/Find_A_Good_Breeder

standard poodle and is around 55 centimetres tall. My husband and I viewed both parents when we visited Manchester. We were able to see instantly that both were in good health and were reasonably calm animals. Where possible it's best to ask to see both parents in order to check the health for yourself. If the vendor refuses it may be wise to question why; they may have an underlying motive for their refusal. These particular pups were kept in spacious conditions and were very contented, it was plain to see. I was happy to make a choice from this litter.

We looked at all six puppies in the litter and I fell in love with every single with one them! Some were brown, two were black and one was amber coloured. Finally we chose our boy: a little black bundle of fluff, fur and energy. He was as cute as anything you've ever seen, sent to steal everyone's hearts!

We called him Noodles simply because his hair was reminiscent of a bowl of noodles. It wasn't poodle curly and it wasn't schnauzer straight, it was like a bowl of bendy noodles. Our boy had a name. We thought it might also be an easy name for the children with speech and language challenges to master. One week down the line we realised that a puppy's name needs a hard sound at the beginning to draw his attention when you are attempting to give him instructions. Noodles became Doodles as it is easier to sound firmer and as though you are in control of the situation rather than the puppy when the name starts with a hard sound. We also discovered that Doodles is the name of the dog from the television programme 'The Tweenies'. It hadn't been our intention to name him after a children's television animal but it certainly didn't do any harm as the younger children were able to identify with him.

Once we had him at home it became a whirlwind of buying all things puppy related. I had a week to have the puppy settled in at home before taking him to school and introducing him to the children. Doodles was 11 weeks old and needed to be a fast learner.

There was one matter which needed attending to before I could think of taking Doodles into school for the first time: the purchase of his blue collar and lead. These two items were chosen specifically as was his name tag so that he would be in the same colours as the children's school uniform. Consistency is important for all children and our special children needed to be able to identify Doodles with the school colours. Doodles now had his preliminary kit and was able to make his first visit to school during that half term.

Chapter 4

INTRODUCING OUR PUPPY TO SCHOOL

So, during the holidays I took the opportunity to take Doodles into school for his first look around. This was the one and only time that the little pup was ever nervous. Now we are a few months down the line I can report that nervousness and anxiety do not form part of his personality! After a discussion with our headteacher it was decided that Doodles would share my office and would be crate trained for his own benefit. Once in school he would need his own safe haven away from the children where he could take himself to have some peace and quiet. This is exactly what he has at home and he likes the security of having his own safe space. During those first few days my husband and I made my office Doodles ready. In came the crate, the water bowl, the chewy sticks and an assortment of brightly coloured, noisy toys all ready to cater to the every whim of an 11-week-old schnoodle puppy.

Toilet training was a concern for me. At home we had attempted to train him with puppy pads, all to no avail. Our mischievous boy dispensed with them rather quickly by ripping them to pieces and covering our lounge with their contents. A different solution was needed for that problem. My husband devised the puppy pack and I highly recommend anyone starting on this journey make up their own puppy packs. Each one consisted of an absorbent square of cloth, a detergent wet wipe and a throw away plastic glove all encased in a sandwich bag. These are quick and easy to make in advance and can be disposed of after the offending puddle has been dealt with. Brilliant!

That first visit to school was also Doodles' first encounter with Rosie our headteacher. It was vital that he endeared himself to her straight away as otherwise he might have had the shortest career of any school dog ever! That is exactly what he did. He made sure that she loved him right from the beginning. He sat beautifully on her knee as though he was perfectly trained to do so. He was incredibly well behaved and didn't once attempt to eat any of her beautiful plants, not on that occasion anyway!

The first day of the new half term arrived and it was INSET day. Doodles was formally introduced by Rosie at our whole school briefing as our latest member of staff. At this point the dog was a complete surprise to most people. She told everyone that he would be on the school premises all the time during the school week (although for most of the time he would be with me in my office) and would eventually join in lessons with the children. He now is around the children on average for 30 minutes a day, split throughout the day. The news went down a treat and everyone was on board with the idea of Highfurlong's own school dog, especially one as cute as Doodles.

That Monday morning briefing was when I first realised that we may have a slight problem with Doodles and the staff. They came from all over the school to play with him and to spoil him. He had presents of cuddly teddies and chewy sticks brought in for him. Several of the teaching assistants took him outside for his regular constitutional and threw a ball for him. Under their watchful eye he chased leaves and anything that moved and they let him jump all over them as he grew more and more excited with his new friends. He was having a truly wonderful time and he hadn't even come across a single child yet.

The next day was the day Doodles was formally introduced to the children. In came the children and I gradually began to take him around the classes. All the children wanted to hold him and stroke him and cuddle him. He began to work his own special brand of magic on the children immediately.

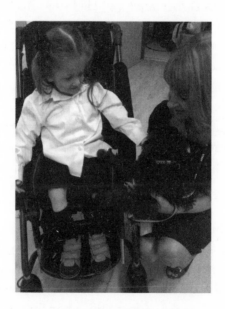

I slowly moved from classroom to classroom carrying the wriggling little puppy. We caused total chaos wherever we went. Everyone wanted to touch him and pet him. Doodles of course lapped up all the attention. He was in seventh heaven. I knew right there and then that some kind of rota was going to be required. All of the children, all of the classes, were going to want him to be with them and he couldn't be everywhere at once. Also, he needed lots of sleep as he was still very young. I needed to give this matter some thought. For now, all that mattered was that he was in school and he was accepted by everyone. Not one single person or child had a bad word to say.

Each morning a trail of people came to my office – not to see me but to see Doodles. I became the most popular yet the most ignored member of staff in school, such was his puppy power.

Right from the very beginning the staff loved him, after all, who doesn't love a puppy? He brings his own special brand of magic to the school. He has many firm friends among the staff. It was with the staff that we first realised there were some unintended, unexpected but very welcome aspects to having a dog in school. For example, one of our teaching assistants has fought and beaten cancer twice and this has given her a completely different outlook on life. Andrea now appreciates that life is too short for not doing the things that make you happy. She adores Doodles and tells me that she finds him calming and therapeutic. If she feels at all down she comes for a Doodles' cuddle. She takes him for a 20-minute walk every morning and a 20-minute walk during her own lunch time in all kinds of weather. Andrea enjoys walking but her illness has left her with epilepsy and she doesn't feel confident to go for walks alone. Doodles is the perfect companion for her. She treats him by bringing him doggy biscuits and chewy sticks. He also has the cleanest bedding of any puppy in the land as she washes his blanket regularly. She dries him off after his walk if the weather is inclement and thoroughly spoils him. In return Doodles brings her a bar of chocolate every so often to say thank you for all the attention she showers on him.

The next person who is a firm favourite with Doodles is Bridget, our school secretary. Bridget is a very poorly lady indeed. You wouldn't know it from looking at the permanent smile on her face. Bridget certainly knows how to put a brave face on for the world. Without going into too much detail she struggles to walk and wears wrist and knee splints. She is only able to work part time due to her illness and that is quite depressing for someone who is relatively young. Doodles runs into the office and throws himself on to Bridget's lap. He showers her with kisses and gives her the biggest puppy cuddle ever seen. He would sit with Bridget all day long if I let him. Bridget allows him to chew the cardboard boxes when they are finished with and sometimes he's even allowed to open them! Bridget has bought him special toys for the office. He has his own cuddly monkey to chew when he's in there. He's such a spoilt puppy! Bridget tells me that she loves her cuddles with Doodles and he really makes her smile on the days when she feels particularly unwell.

It has to be said that Doodles is well loved by the staff and I hadn't anticipated the extent of this at all. Another person that Doodles has won over is our headteacher. He has shown that he is no respecter of authority whatsoever. When our head comes into my room and sits down, up jumps Doodles. He's as quick as a flash, rather mischievous and there's no stopping him. He's quite partial to her ears and washes them both for her. There's nothing you can do except laugh because he's so cheeky. Our headteacher attempts to be firm with him but it falls on deaf ears as he carries on washing her face for her. It's a good job she likes him or he could be our very first exclusion!

So, it's safe to say that Doodles has been good for staff morale. Right from day one there was a 'feel-good factor' around the school whenever Doodles was around. He was very mischievous in those early days and that seemed only to add to his charm. One example of this was when our school secretary was in my office returning some papers to me. As it was 'dress down Friday' Claudia was wearing a lovely pair of distressed jeans. Doodles took an instant liking to these and decided that they ought to be further distressed. Before we realised what he was up to he had the torn part around the knee in his mouth and was beginning to pull hard! Any second we would have heard the sound of tearing denim except she realised and we stopped him. It was difficult to keep the smile from our faces and even more difficult to admonish him. Although Claudia did reveal that her mum would have loved Doodles as she is no fan of her distressed jeans.

Once Doodles had been in school for a few weeks and was gaining in confidence I needed a way to slow him down. From the start he had a winning way with the children and was incredibly gentle with them. He simply seemed to know that they are special children and that he couldn't jump on them, pull them around or cause them to be troubled in any way at all. Not so with me! He seemed to think that he could run down the corridor with me in tow almost flying along behind him. He refused to walk calmly for me yet he had a special talent with the children. I needed to get him a harness; that was the key to making him walk sedately by my side. A blue harness was purchased and then I took it to a very clever cobbler who stitched the school's logo onto it for me. My goodness my puppy looked smart! He sat very proudly in his blue school uniform to have his picture taken and there isn't a trace of mischief in his face at all!

— Chapter 5 —

PRACTICALITIES AND FINANCES

This chapter deals with the practical issues of the puppy and the finances associated with him. I will deal with the money aspects first as this is always a thorny issue. The first task when thinking about introducing a dog is who is going to pay for it. In the case of our school our headteacher was more than happy that school should pay as the children were the ones who were going to reap the benefits of having him in school each day. I gave this matter a great deal of thought and came to a decision that suited everyone. I would pay for the dog and he would be my dog, I would take him home each evening and in the holidays and he would come into work every day with me. My reasons were purely practical. For example, what would happen if I became unwell and needed to be off school for a few weeks? If the dog had been purchased by school I would then have a duty and responsibility to the school to have him sent into work each day. That would be difficult to achieve. Also, if I was to take him each night and at weekends as if he was my dog what would happen if another staff member wanted to take him home with them? I would have no objections to this but I'm not sure it would be fair to the puppy as he needs one home with one family where he can be truly settled. For teachers in a similar position in other schools you also need to think what would happen if you wanted to change schools. If you were fortunate enough to gain a promotion and you were the keeper of the school dog, would you then lose your dog? If school had purchased the dog you would almost certainly have to hand him over to someone else and that could be traumatic. For me this wasn't a consideration, as I have no intention of leaving my present school. Most of the financial decisions regarding Doodles were easy. I would foot the bill and the children would have their pet. My trip to a well-known pet shop saw me purchase two of everything, which was quite expensive, but it was worth it for my own peace of mind. No matter what the future held, Doodles would be mine but the headteacher and I were determined that our little pup's work place would literally be a home from home.

The next consideration was his behaviour. When he was a tiny puppy he was relatively easy to control and was very willing to please. He would do anything for the treat of a dog biscuit. As he grew older he became more wilful and wanted everything his own way. If he wanted to run around the dining hall at top speed ignoring all the commands for him to stop, then he would do! If he wanted to walk across my computer to gain my attention while I was typing, he would do! I would remove him to the floor and tell him to stay and by the time I had sat at my desk again he was on my chair with me. He could jump like a pole vaulter! I'm sure that in another place at another time this could be very useful but not in a school setting. I needed to do something. Puppy training classes were the answer. I enrolled him for weekly sessions on Tuesday evenings at the local puppy classes. Once there he was the star of the show. He could sit, walk, leave, wait and do pretty much anything while the dog trainer was there. She told me that he was suited to agility classes as he's very quick to learn, very fast and very agile. What she didn't know was that away from classes when it was just Doodles and me he continued to be a minx. For others he was far better behaved, which does lead me to question if I am too soft with him. Either way, all pups should attend training classes. Your dog will be happier in a routine and if he understands what you want him to do. It also helps them to socialise with other dogs and lots of humans in an environment similar to a classroom, which is handy for a school dog in training.

Next you need to consider having a policy in place for the dog. I have documented the benefits of introducing a dog into school and these are many. There seems to be little dispute that dogs are good for children as long as they are calm and well behaved. It is common sense that there should still be a risk assessment and a policy in place. The policy should show who owns the dog, if it's hypoallergenic, what type of dog it is and where it will live. The policy should also contain details of the dog's temperament and who will pay any veterinary bills incurred. It should also state that people new to the school will be informed of the dog's presence. The policy should have clear rules around the dog's day-to-day management. For example, Doodles' policy says that he will be supervised by an adult at all times, kept on a lead unless being exercised outside, stay at home if he is unwell, be fully crate trained and be fully inoculated and regularly wormed. The policy goes on to say that children and young people will not have sole responsibility for Doodles and will be regularly reminded that they have a duty not to over excite the dog. Our school policy also reminds children not to allow Doodles to lick their faces, not to wake him when he is asleep, not to feed him human food, not to put their faces next to his and to wash their hands after playing with him or handling him. Further to that we have also added some general health and safety principles. These include encouraging children to walk and play calmly around Doodles, to not encourage him to jump up and to take regular exercise with the dog and the supervising adult. The policy will be reviewed annually and will be added to as a work in progress as Doodles continues his training.

Similarly you will need to have a risk assessment in place. This should cover the hazards arising from having the dog in school and the precautions you have put in place to combat these. For example, the hazards could include dog faeces and urine causing illness or falls. The precautions will include cleaning up any dog mess immediately after an accident has occurred and disposing of it in a hygienic place. The staff member must also wash their hands immediately after carrying out this task. Another hazard might include an allergic reaction to the dog. The precaution will be to purchase a dog which does not moult and is hypoallergenic such as a schnoodle or a cockapoo. The dog's bedding will be kept clean at all times and the dog will be groomed weekly or as required. If a child is allergic to the dog then close contact with the dog will be prohibited.

Obviously the ultimate risk with having a dog in school comes from a bite or a scratch. The precaution is to purchase a dog like Doodles that is bred for being calm and sociable. These dogs are well known for being very good around children and Doodles seems to have an innate ability to know when a child is very delicate. Even when he was just three months old he seemed to know that some of our very special children needed a very delicate touch. He was incredibly gentle with them and snuggled his nose into their hands to give them the sensory experience of being close to a puppy. A further precaution is that children should never be alone with the dog to prevent any incidents occurring. Also, as mentioned, our school policy states that Doodles will always be on his lead when he is in the corridors or around the children. It will not matter how much we come to trust him in later years, this will always be a condition of him being in school to ensure the safety of our children. As humans we can never say with absolute certainty that the dog is totally trustworthy and it's a chance we aren't willing to take. For this reason the supervising adult will always check the dog is not being over-stimulated or becoming anxious. The adult in charge will be responsible for removing Doodles to his own safe place if there is a sign that he is being over-stimulated or over-excited. The risk assessment and the policy are both quite clear that Doodles will not be with the children for more than 15 minutes at a time. This is to safeguard the dog's well-being. He loves being with the children but we must ensure he has regular breaks and is well cared for.

The last hazard I will mention is that there is a small danger that a third party could sue the school if they were injured by the dog. This risk should not be taken lightly. Schools should check their insurance policies and ensure the dog is covered. After conducting some research I have discovered that some local authorities already provide extra cover for schools with dogs. Our school has taken out added third party liability insurance to ensure we are covered in the unlikely event of Doodles nibbling or injuring anyone in any way.

Chapter 6

THE DOG'S INTENDED REMIT IN SCHOOL

When I first thought about introducing a dog for our school I had in mind a certain set of activities I wanted the dog to participate in. Most of what I had in mind was therapeutic. I envisaged him being used for cuddles and snuggles for children who had fallen over or for children who were emotionally hurt from some childish squabble. I thought he might be there to comfort those who are incredibly poorly and need to rest and I thought he might be able to help our children relax. Children who face debilitating medical challenges are exhausted for much of the time and I envisaged Doodles being there for them when they needed a warm, soft embrace. Of course this is exactly what he has done. He is always willing to go and work with the children. He gives fantastic puppy cuddles and he loves to run around with those who are able.

I also thought that part of his remit would involve him being used as a reward for children who have worked hard. He could be one of their choices to help them remain on task throughout a lesson. Again this is a vision that has been realised. If children have a successful lesson they may earn a certificate and a set amount of time with Doodles.

Not only is this a popular reward it is also an excellent incentive for those children who love the dog.

I envisaged Doodles having a large part to play with children with behaviour challenges. This is one part of his role where he has been especially effective. For some children it has been written into their behaviour for learning plans that if they earn a set amount of points they are allowed to have Doodles' cuddles or to play with him as a reward. I also envisaged him being able to encourage children to sit quietly in lessons and listen to their teacher. Much of this was his intended remit and he has achieved all of this and more.

Right from the beginning our little pup exceeded all expectations. He was excellent in performing all the activities on his remit, although he did struggle to keep himself calm sometimes, especially when he was very young. Cuddles are now very calming although he may still be a little excitable at times. This in itself has a therapeutic effect as his behaviour often makes the children laugh. As we all know a distressed child benefits from laughter being the best medicine of all.

As soon as Doodles was old enough he received his very first timetable. This was a first draft and was devised by Erica, one of our rather talented Level 4 teaching assistants. It is intended to evolve with him as he grows in maturity. His day begins when he is dressed in his school uniform, a harness bearing the school's 'Highfurlong' logo. He waits patiently at the door of my office to greet all the staff who walk my way and lots of puppy licks and frolics occur as he makes everyone smile right from the moment they enter the school building. In reality he's waiting for one person, Andrea, who takes him for his 20-minute walk whatever the weather and he adores her for that treat.

Doodles' day begins in earnest at 9 a.m. when the school transport begins to arrive carrying all our children for school. He is changed into his dayglo jacket which exactly matches the coat of the site supervisor Mr Tinkler who organises the car park. His jacket also bears the 'Highfurlong' logo as consistency is paramount for many of our children. Changing Doodles into his outdoor gear is not an easy task I might add; more of that tale later. Once he has his coat on he sets off with Mr Tinkler wagging his tail quite happily. The children adore catching a first glimpse of Doodles as he welcomes them into school and they wave at him and tap on their bus windows. The knock-on effect of this early morning encounter is that our children begin their day with a smile on their faces before they have even alighted from their buses.

Once all the children are safely inside school Doodles once again takes up his position in my office to see what the day will hold. This is where his timetable comes into play. His timetable exactly matches the visual timetable that we use for our children. Consistency is key for our youngsters and they need to see that Doodles has to stick to a similar pattern and a similar set of rules just as they do. His timetable is attached to my door in order that the children are able to see where he is at any time and they will know that he is not always available for them personally.

His first encounter is usually a 15-year-old young man who is on the autism spectrum. This young man finds many everyday occurrences to be a real challenge. Some days he arrives in school and is distressed for reasons which we are not party to and which are out of our control. Sometimes even his mum has no idea what is bothering her son but he is not actually 'school ready' at that moment in time. Luckily, we have the perfect antidote for this situation and Doodles is on hand to assist. He goes up to the young man who may be feeling very angry with the world and he sits in front of him and waits patiently while the young man runs his hands up and down Doodles' back. The boy loves the feel of the schnoodle's soft, comforting fur. Doodles licks his hand and the boy just can't help but smile. In an instant all his troubles seem to melt away. You can actually see the distressed veil lifting from his face as he visibly calms down. He is now ready to join his peers in class. On occasions this young man may become upset during the school day. Loud noises or unexpected events may make him anxious and he may show some signs of not being able to cope in the classroom. In a situation like that he will ask to visit our calming sensory room for a period of chilling out and restoring his inner peace. When that happens Doodles often joins him and speeds up the healing process. Our puppy loves working with this young man and in turn the boy responds well to Doodles' loving care and attention.

The next daily occurrence is the arrival of Fay, a four-year-old girl who has a rare genetic disease and fights a continuing battle to beat her physical challenges. At the moment Fay is just taking her very first independent steps. She uses anything she can to steady herself and is very determined that she will be able to walk. The only thing holding her back just now is the fear factor. She is afraid that she will fall and hurt herself. Physiotherapists have given her a hula hoop to hold on to with an adult holding the other side. This is working well and she is making progress. One day, with help from a special support assistant she happened to walk past my office and spotted Doodles. She plonked herself down on the floor and refused to move until she had stroked and patted the pup. It was at that point that Paula, the teaching assistant who was with Fay, realised that she utterly adores Doodles and quite possibly he could be used as an incentive for her to walk. What a brilliant idea! On went his lead, up stood Fay and began to walk with one hand holding the wall and one hand holding his lead. These were very slow and tentative steps to begin with but Fay was absolutely thrilled to bits with herself. Doodles was very young so Paula held his lead at the same time to ensure the little girl was safe and not pulled over if the puppy became too boisterous. This was sheer magic to observe and I have to admit to feeling a little emotional when I saw the little girl walking the puppy down the corridor. This was then written into his timetable. Each morning, Doodles and Fay take their exercise together and her little legs are growing stronger for the experience. This is a bonus we hadn't envisaged.

The next thing scheduled on Doodles' timetable is to take exercise with Key Stage 5. As anyone who has any experience of teenagers knows it's nigh on impossible to separate them from their technology. Each young person has an iPad or a computer or some kind of technology and they refuse to be parted from it. After all, what self-respecting 17-year-old wants to run up and down and burn off some energy? Introduce a puppy into that scenario and everything changes in an instant. Suddenly they were queuing up to take the puppy on to the grass. I had to actually limit his exercise at one point for fear of him being worn to a frazzle. Doodles of course lapped up all the attention. He was having the best time possible and was loving his role in school. One of the teachers designed a certificate for children and young people who helped to exercise him. If they came regularly to run around with him they earned the title 'Champion Dog Walker'. Well of course this brand new certificate with a puppy's picture on it was well worth having and encouraged the children to come and take him on the grass.

As mentioned in our policy, I had to programme in several sessions for Doodles to have a sleep. My office is the place where he spends the majority of his day and I had to ensure he was well rested. He will keep going all day long until he collapses in a heap. In those early days the children had to learn that part of having a pet was caring for it and tending to its every need. Once Doodles was fed, watered and exercised the children had to learn that he had to have some down time. He needed rest just as they did. Some children weren't aware of this and produced one or two strops and sulks to begin with but they realised that if they wanted to play with him he had to have rest breaks too. This was a valuable lesson for the children.

In the beginning the afternoons were when I allowed Doodles to accompany me to lessons. He had his own blanket, supplied by Key Stage 5, and he had to lie on it while the older students were having their computing lessons. The plan was that if they paid attention all the way through the lesson and produced their finest work they would be allowed to take Doodles out into the courtyard to play. This was all the incentive they needed. All heads would go down and they worked incredibly well and off they went with the excited puppy in tow. Another successful session thanks to Doodles.

At the end of the day Doodles is once more dressed in his dayglo jacket and is taken out to the car park to see the children safely off the premises. Just as at the beginning of the day the children stop and say goodbye to him and stroke him. They knock on the windows of their buses and wave to him as they are driven away. It is always a good sight to see smiling children and young people at the end of the school day.

— Chapter 7 —

DOODLES' SUCCESS

Extracurricular

So that was Doodles' intended remit at the start of his school career. His timetable was to be revised as he became older, calmer and more sensible. In time we wanted to include him being used as a reading dog to encourage reluctant readers. At first there was a massive problem with that plan; Doodles was too young and couldn't be trusted around the books. On his inaugural attempt at being a reading dog he sat patiently for a few minutes listening to a young girl read. Then he shuffled ever closer to the book and the reader. Before another minute had passed his nibbling teeth had wrapped themselves around the book and he began to pull! Doodles was not mature enough to be a reading dog just yet and the attempt was aborted.

In time, we want to introduce him into literacy lessons to support speech and language. Our speech and language therapists can see a very important role for Doodles in encouraging speech and improved vocabulary. We have seen an improvement already with little Fay who began walking to be with Doodles and who can now say 'Doodles' and 'doggy', two words that she couldn't say previously! We also have several children who aren't confident speakers but have begun to say various canine-related words. For us this is a very real and unexpected bonus of having a puppy in school. We knew there would be benefits but we hadn't envisaged just how powerful that child and dog bond could be.

Further down the line we would like to take Doodles on school trips to help children who are nervous or anxious. He is still only nine months old and as yet some of the things we would like him to be a part of are not a reality due to his young age. What we hadn't envisaged was just how gentle Doodles would be around our very poorly and special children. We hoped he would be gentle, but the bond that we have witnessed has been incredible. The first time Doodles heard a child cry he cocked his head on one side and listened intently. He must have wondered what the strange sound was. I put him on his lead and off we went to find the child who was crying. It was a little girl from our Early Years class. She was very young and wasn't feeling too well. She had been lifted from her buggy and was sitting on the lap of one of the teaching assistants for comfort. Doodles and I entered the interactive sensory room where the child was and we carefully and quietly moved towards her. I didn't want to startle her or make her tears worse by introducing the puppy if she didn't even like dogs. I actually had no real idea whether Doodles might help but considered it worth a try. Doodles went up to her and pushed his cold, wet nose into her hand. She stopped crying instantly to see what had touched her hand. In a flash of recognition, she realised that the puppy was right in front of her. She reached out her other hand and tugged at his fur. Our little pup simply allowed her to do it. It was almost as though he knew this was his job and he was going to do it well. For my part I was worried. I had him on a very short lead and my hand was right next to his mouth because I had no idea how he was going to react to having his fur pulled by the little girl. I was taking no chances at all. He sat there and simply licked her hand and allowed her to tug on his ears until she squealed with laughter. We were very careful to make sure she didn't hurt him but we were extremely pleased to see that he had stopped her from crying and more than that he had actually made her giggle. This was his first encounter with a distressed child and he passed the test with flying colours. Ever since that first encounter with tears whenever Doodles hears a child crying he puts his head on one side to listen and goes to the door in anticipation of finding the child who needs him. Clever dog!

In reality this caring role has been where Doodles has had more success than we anticipated. Whenever a child is distressed, for whatever reason, I'm often called on to take Doodles and attempt to cheer up the child or young person. The reason could be due to a falling over resulting in a scuffed knee or arm, or a disagreement with another child resulting in tears, or it could be for something entirely different. Some of our children are exceptionally poorly and occasionally may experience a seizure. When the child has recovered from this but is still not ready to rejoin their class Doodles may be called upon to give a therapeutic cuddle. On a similar theme if a child isn't feeling very well for any reason a little fresh air might just be required. Doodles is of course happy to help out with this request. He will always take a trip outside with the children. Arguments between children are his speciality! If we hear an argument Doodles and I arrive on the scene armed with a ball to be thrown outside. The argument is soon forgotten when there is a puppy with a ball frolicking in front of the children. When all is calm we take five minutes outside and diffuse the situation. Doodles plays with the squabbling children and administers cuddles as required. For his part he is more than happy to help out; he can't receive enough cuddles, he just loves them.

Another unexpected bonus from having a school dog happened at Christmas. Christmas is a time of the year when many children struggle to cope with the daily routine of school. School is their safe haven away from home. It is the place where they have learnt to trust people other than their parents and to know that those people will always have their best interests at heart. At Christmas time the cracks begin to appear for the children and some just can't cope. There's a very good reason for that: the routine they need and cherish so much in schools disappears out of the window at Christmas time. Teachers and teaching assistants have the best intentions; they try their hardest to ensure that anxious children will manage their day without experiencing a full blown meltdown or become so anxious that they retreat into themselves. For most children Christmas is a time of joy, excitement, presents and laughter. They are allowed to watch festive films at the end of term, listen to music, play with iPads and generally have some 'down time' for the last day or two in school. It's the most magical time of the entire year to be in school, filled with anticipation and dreams of what Santa might bring.

For other children it's a time of absolute despair. Each new day brings a new activity that isn't on that visual timetable. Some neurotypical children are not happy with this lack of structure but for children like some of ours who are living with challenges such as ADHD and ASC Christmas is an incredibly challenging time. For example, if a child or young person has ASC quite often the problem is in the child's understanding and communication skills.

Although they may be verbal, they sometimes prefer not to join in a conversation and prefer to be alone. Children with ASC often have sensory issues such as being irritated by the feeling of certain clothing, may only eat certain foods and have a fear of loud noises and crowds that sends them into a sheer panic. There may also be some real temper issues due to a lack of understanding of what is required of them.

Imagine being a child who has a dual diagnosis of ADHD and ASC and it is easy to see how they might struggle at this time of the year. A child like this would be totally swamped by being in a crowd; they might feel positively ill from being around all the different food smells at this time of year and may be sent into absolute panic at the complete lack of structure and routine. Their normal class staff may disappear for any number of reasons and the child in question who has no sense of danger may remove themselves from the room without telling anyone. It's a lonely time for this child too. Everyone else is laughing and having fun and loving all the changes; our child might just have taken themselves off to what they think is a safe space but may in reality be a dangerous place for them.

In our school we have a 14-year-old girl who has this dual diagnosis. Like many schools up and down the country we suspend our lessons for the week prior to the Christmas show in order to rehearse. Every single child and young person takes part in this show irrespective of the challenges or illnesses they face. The vast majority absolutely love performing for their parents and they love all the rehearsals. It is a wonderful sight to see everyone singing and dancing on stage and able-bodied children helping those with more severe medical challenges to join in. It brings a tear to your eye if I'm honest.

One day in the run up to the show I went to watch the rehearsals. As I'm assistant head and I don't have my own class I don't often get the chance to see the rehearsals and as today was a whole school run through I popped up to have a look. The sound of singing met me in the corridor so I was looking forward to it before I was anywhere near it. As I approached it I could hear a raised voice. A 14-year-old girl simply wasn't going in. She was shouting, thumping her fists and banging her feet on the floor and expressing her dislike. Very soon she was on her feet and about to take flight. Her problem as I'm sure you've guessed was sensory overload. There was just too much noise, too many people and too much going on in a confined space. Our girl couldn't see any way she could cope with this and was expressing herself in the only way she knew how: with a sensory meltdown. To the untrained eye, this would appear as a behaviour issue and result in sanctions. To those who understand it was quite apparent what was happening. I took her to a quiet part of the corridor and waited until she was calm enough to listen. 'Shall we go and get Doodles?' She looked at me questioningly. I told her that Doodles needed to get used to loud noises and be desensitised around crowds and that she and the school pup could sit right at the back where we could take him out if it became too much for him. It took her a few minutes before she agreed and off we went to fetch Doodles. As promised we sat at the back where we could beat a hasty retreat if needed. After a short time our girl and our puppy had moved right up to the centre of the hall. She was able to cope with her own sensory issues because she was helping the puppy to cope with his. She was blotting out all her sensory problems as she concentrated on Doodles. That was a good day. Doodles had worked his magic on this young girl and had saved the day. This was a welcome but unexpected bonus of having Doodles.

Christmas also brought further benefits that we hadn't anticipated. For example, Christmas cards began to be delivered to my office in large numbers. This is not an unusual occurrence for teachers so I didn't really concern myself with them at first. When I gathered them up at the end of the first day I realised that none of the cards were for me, they were for Doodles! I felt slightly side-lined by the pup but I soon got over it as I looked at the writing. These children had spent their weekend doing their best writing and drawing pictures for Doodles on the cards. He may not have been too impressed but I certainly was. There was a marked improvement in some of the handwriting from the children. Maybe they thought he would be able to read it if they wrote neatly, who knows, but it was lovely to see. Doodles also received a couple of Christmas presents from the children. They had spent their own pocket money buying him doggy chewing sticks and treats and wrapped up the presents for him. He was one very lucky dog. The children adored seeing him rip off the paper and it was a bonus to see this caring side from the children come to the fore.

As time has progressed Doodles is becoming quite famous in his own right. He is well known in the local area and I am often stopped while people ask me if he is Highfurlong's school dog. Some of this can be attributed to the drivers and escorts on the transport who bring the children into school. They have been exceptionally encouraging about Doodles and have enjoyed following his progress. They talk to the children on the buses about the puppy and they have told me that the children use animated language when discussing Doodles with them.

When I take him outside for his afternoon toilet stop just as the buses arrive the drivers and escorts alight from their transport and come over and ask about his progress. Some of them have treats for him in their pockets. Doodles is very happy to be fussed by the transport staff and waits patiently for a biscuit. The drivers and escorts tell their friends about Doodles and I have had several telephone and email enquiries from other teachers in the area about his role in school. This is an unexpected bonus of having Doodles and it is always a pleasure to be involved in helping other teachers and schools to progress. On a similar theme I have been able to help numerous people on Twitter with advice about buying a school dog and the pitfalls and benefits of doing so. We have had three visitors to school from educators on Twitter who have read my blog posts and who have requested to see him in action. Doodles is more than happy to rise to the occasion.

Chapter 8

DOODLES WITH CHILDREN

Case Studies

I have given some indication of the success that Doodles was having with the children and young people but there are several children who have especially benefitted from being around the puppy.[1]

LILY

One of these is Lily who is now 14 years old. Lily is one of the most adorable young people you could ever wish to meet. She will do anything for anyone and is very willing to please. She is never happier than when something has gone right in her world and she can command the whole school to 'clap'. However, Lily is terrified of dogs. At the time of bringing Doodles into school I was unaware of this fact. One morning while on our patrol around the corridors Doodles and I happened upon Lily. She jumped backwards and was visibly shaken. I removed the excited puppy from

---

1   Children's names have been changed.

the area and Lily continued on her journey to collect the register. All the time she was chatting away and saying her version of 'Doodles, Doodles!' at the top of her voice. He had made an impression on her but I wasn't sure if this was a good or bad impression. The next day Lily walked past my office and peeped in. She is not a confident speaker but managed to make me understand that she wanted to see the pup. I popped him on his lead in a vague attempt to keep him calm and I encouraged her to come close to him. She was with a special support assistant at the time who gently nudged the puppy and the girl ever closer together. Lily desperately wanted to touch the puppy and kept holding her hand out for him to kiss her but as soon as he came close to her she pulled back. She was disappointed with herself and pushed her hand towards him again but she wasn't quite brave enough. This happened for a few days until one day Lily put her hand out and held it steady. The support assistant and I held our breath and the young pup instinctively knew he had to be gentle. That day was to be a turning point for Lily. Although she wasn't brave enough to stroke him on that occasion she was in very close proximity with him and she had allowed him to lick her hand. After a few days it became part of Lily's routine to collect the register and pop in and say hello to Doodles. Before the week was out she was brave enough to stroke him. When she touched his curly puppy fur she exclaimed that it 'tickled' and burst into fits of giggles. Fast forward a couple of months and Lily now collects Doodles at the door with her support assistant and holds the dog's lead and walks him to collect the register. The first time she insisted on holding his lead I was very worried. He was still very exuberant and I was anxious that he might pull her over. I attempted to hold the lead alongside Lily but she wouldn't allow that. She wanted to be in charge. I found out later from Lily's mum that she had a bad experience with a dog some years earlier and had almost run into the road to escape from the animal. Her mum was very impressed that she had overcome her fears and was actually walking the dog around school. This is a brilliant example of the benefits of having a dog in school.

MASON

Another little boy who loves having Doodles in school is Mason who is ten years old. Mason is a real cheeky character and is unable to walk. He maintains his independence around school by using his arms to manoeuvre his wheelchair and propel himself wherever he wishes to go. Mason also finds talking and expressing his needs rather a challenge. Like all children he doesn't always want to be independent. He would rather someone push him around sometimes but it is important that he remains independent. Our school is designed especially for our children and young people. It is all on the ground floor and it is designed in a rectangle so that staff and pupils can go either way around the building as the fancy takes them. One of the ways around the rectangular circuit is much longer from where Mason's classroom is based. Each day at lunchtime he is supposed to propel himself the longer way around the building in order to reach the dining hall. Just sometimes he doesn't feel like doing that. Like everyone else he has his tired days and tries to take the short route or even be pushed to the hall. Maintaining his strength in his upper arms is vital for his future independence so staff have to be firm and insist that he takes the longer route. My office is situated on the longer route. Suddenly we no longer have a problem encouraging him to take the long way around. First of all he stops every day at our headteacher's door and says hello to her. He tells her it's his dinner time and carries on to the room next door. He pushes open the door and shouts to Doodles who is more than happy to bound over and see him. Doodles stands on his back two paws and puts his front two on Mason's knee. He lets the little lad stroke and cuddle him. For his part, Mason is learning new vocabulary. He can call the dog over and say hello to him and with a little support he can ask questions about what Doodles has been doing. This improved speech and language is a real bonus for him and for us as staff.

RICKY

The next child who is benefitting from having Doodles around is Ricky. He is only six years old and has a smile to melt your heart. He cannot walk at all and cannot propel himself independently. He is unable to talk and uses a specialised speech and language aid known as a PODD book to help him to express his wishes. He relies on an adult for all his needs but most definitely knows his own mind. He loves it when I take Doodles into his class for a quarter of an hour every Thursday morning. He laughs and giggles at the pup's antics and it seems that Doodles rises to the occasion to make Ricky giggle. For example, in the winter Ricky wore a furry hat to keep out the chill. Once Ricky removed his hat from his head it was put safely under his buggy ready for the next time it was needed. Up popped Doodles and pinched the hat. He would throw it up into the air and play with it while lying on his back. He was doing no harm whatsoever to the hat, although it did become a little soggy but it made all the children in

Rectangle Class giggle. For his next trick he once waited until Ricky had been transferred into his classroom chair and when I wasn't looking he jumped into Ricky's buggy. This was the one and only time the puppy was to do this as he was very swiftly and firmly told off but the giggles that came from Ricky were pure magic. Ricky began to encourage the puppy to jump on his knee. It seemed like these two were not a good combination. When Doodles did get very close to him, Ricky often wanted to share his banana with him. It was as if they were encouraging each other to be mischievous! Once again it was a special support assistant who decided to harness this bond and had Ricky and Doodles working together to deliver messages around the school. Never have I seen a little boy look so proud of himself as he holds the dog's lead and delivers messages around the school with his support assistant. Maybe they are a good combination after all.

As time has progressed Ricky has begun to take his first steps around school. This has nothing to do with Doodles as the staff and physiotherapists do all the hard work on this one. They are a great bunch of talented individuals and will use any means at their disposal to help the children to walk or move independently. At the start of March Doodles and I were walking past Ricky as he was sitting in the library area of the school perusing the books. He had been on a mission to deliver the class register to the school office using his walking frame. Part way through his task, on his return to class he had gone on strike and was refusing to move any further. Doodles and I came around the corner and the young boy instantly hauled himself to his feet and stood with the aid of his walking frame. He made it very clear that he wanted to walk Doodles back to class. The support assistant and I had a bit of a struggle in working out how to attach the lead to the frame while leaving enough slack for Ricky to hold it, but after a little head scratching we achieved it. Doodles realised that the boy was in charge and walked slowly back to the classroom, Ricky was beaming from ear to ear! Doodles had done well, enticing the boy to walk back to class without any fuss.

Possibly one of the most heart-warming occasions happened in the early spring. The winter months had dragged on and they seemed to have lasted for ever. Normally by this time of the school year we are able to have the younger children outside enjoying a little spring sunshine. We have extensive grounds at the side of the school and there is an outdoor play area complete with a wheelchair swing and roundabout. The children do enjoy playing out there and of course Doodles loves to be with them. If they are lying down on the grass he thinks he should do the same, although generally he is engaged in attempting to sneak a kiss on someone's hands rather than relaxing in the spring sunshine. The outdoor play area had remained rather water logged and the children were having lunchtime fun in one of the classrooms. On this particular day I took Doodles up to the classroom to see if they wanted to play with him. Ricky, as we have seen, is a big pal of Doodles and he likes to be in charge. He always wants to hold his lead. Ricky was pretending to be a doctor and he cut a very dashing figure wearing his stethoscope around his neck. I told Ricky that if I didn't know better I would confuse him with the real doctor. Once in charge of the lead and Doodles Ricky guided the unsuspecting pup around and made him lie down next to him. I was fascinated to see what was going to happen next. Ricky proceeded to test the dog's heart rate by whipping the stethoscope from around his neck and placing it on the dog's back. He must have decided that this was as close to Doodles' chest as he could get. This was a wise choice because I think if the plastic instrument had been any closer to Doodles' mouth he might have decided it would be a good thing to chew. Once the dog's heart rate had been monitored to Ricky's satisfaction he removed his stethoscope and picked up a pair of doctor's scissors. Obviously these were plastic scissors which was very lucky because Ricky then decided as a result of his tests that the dog's hair needed cutting and he set about performing this minor operation. As a witness to this little scene I can say it was exceedingly cute and also rather funny. The dog had his use as a poorly patient while Ricky mastered his medical training.

ELEANOR

I can report similar success with Eleanor, a six-year-old girl in Rectangle Class. Just like Ricky, Eleanor is starting to take her first tentative steps around school with the help of a walking aid. This is a huge milestone for her and as mobile adults we should never lose sight of the fact that to begin walking at the age of six years must be quite a scary event, even though the children want to gain their independence. Once again, as if by magic Doodles happened to be in the area where young Eleanor was being encouraged to take some steps in a walking frame. We used the dog as an incentive by having him just a few steps in front of her and he wagged his tail furiously as she came closer to him. Eleanor was very pleased with her progress and I had to be very firm with Doodles to prevent him from running up to her because he was very pleased with her progress too! Seeing the bond between the dog and the children makes you realise just how valuable and useful animals can be in our society.

VICTORIA

Several parents are now considering buying puppies as a result of the effect that Doodles has had on their children. For example, Victoria in our Early Years class loves him to bits. She has very little communication and has profound and multiple needs and is therefore sometimes quite a poorly little girl. Doodles can always bring a smile to her face when she is feeling unwell or just when she sees him in the corridor. As with many of our special children, Doodles stands on his back paws and puts his front paws on her knee so that his face is on a level with hers. Victoria loves to be in such close proximity with him and gives him a heart-warming smile. Even though she cannot talk she manages to indicate to her mummy when she has been around Doodles.

FREDDY

Freddy in Rectangle Class who is six years old has not had many dealings with dogs according to his mummy. She was worried that as he grew older he might become scared of dogs especially as he is unable to walk or talk unaided and he has limited sight. As hearing and sighted adults we can only imagine what is going through the mind of a child who cannot see the puppy yet has one close by them all day long. It was important that he was properly introduced to the puppy right from the start and was allowed to touch him, feel his cold nose, count his paws and stroke his curly fur. This is exactly what we did and the boy loved the experience. He gave a beaming grin and his fingers ran all over the dog feeling his soft fur and body and he listened to him panting. After a chat to his mummy about the effect that Doodles has had on her son she is also considering purchasing one. For this little boy the sensory side of the puppy is what pleases him the most. He even loves the noise he makes when he barks. He simply enjoys being around Doodles. You can't really argue with that.

KAYLA

Kayla is in Key Stage 5 and has just turned 18. In many ways she is quite grown up. In other ways she is quite young and needs much nurturing and caring for. Kayla is a wonderful young person who cares deeply about her peers and she tries very hard to be everyone's friend. She also wants to be in charge of everything. If there is a game being played Kayla wants to write the rules and if there is anything happening in Key Stage 5 you can be assured that Kayla is always in the middle of it. As much as Kayla is very popular and loves to lead all the activities she is also sensitive which means she is easily upset. This was apparent on the first day back after the Christmas holidays, which turned out to be an eventful day for Doodles. He was very pleased to be back with the children and young people and was ecstatic when the older girls came into my room in the morning to say hello and to stroke him. Monday's first activity is always an assembly, a welcome to the week type of affair for the whole school. I went along to the assembly to wish everyone a happy new year. Almost immediately I could see that Kayla wasn't too happy. Her body language betrayed her as did the tears rolling down her face. She was really quite upset. After assembly I asked her if a Doodles cuddle would help her and she replied that it definitely would. The two of us went off together to find her furry friend. As soon as she saw him she settled herself on the floor with Doodles and snuggled right into him. He wasn't complaining as he loves a good snuggle. Her tears soon disappeared and Kayla was then able to tell me that she was upset because her own dog was going to have her leg operated on and she was understandably worried about her. As usual Doodles did his job and performed his magic and she was soon recovered and full of her usual smiles. Doodles and I escorted her back to class and she was ready to begin her day.

At break time Kayla returned with her friend Grace and they went off to exercise Doodles. I was standing close by as the three of them ran around full of energy despite the freezing January weather. Just as it was time to go in the girls bent to attach Doodles to his lead when a seagull flew overhead. It deposited several rather large dollops of seagull droppings which narrowly missed the girls and myself. Doodles had the tiniest bit on his black fur. The girls were helpless with laughter at how we had all managed to escape the great seagull dollop and Doodles hadn't. To their great delight they were then able to help me give him a quick wash before returning to class. There was now no trace of Kayla's earlier tears. Doodles had cured her although some of it was unintentional. After this episode Doodles decided to sleep for the rest of the morning and took up residence in the headteacher's chair in my room.

GRACE

Grace is another one of our Key Stage 5 students and like her friend Kayla is quite grown up in many ways. Grace adores Doodles and the feeling is mutual. Most mornings Grace is in school before the rest of the children and is the first young person to see Doodles each day. When he sees her he bounds up to her and stands on his back paws and puts his front paws around her shoulders as though he is encircling her in a real cuddle. His tail wags fast and furious and causes a real draught as he is so pleased to see her. He snuggles right in and tries to shower her with kisses. Obviously for hygiene reasons we don't allow the dog to lick the children's faces but with Doodles I have to be very quick. He is determined that she is having a sloppy Doodles kiss each time he sees her. On Tuesday afternoons Grace is in my Entry Level ICT group and she is quite knowledgeable about this subject. She works very hard in those lessons because she has an incentive to do so. When her work is finished she is allowed to take Doodles outside into the courtyard and she and the pup play together with Grace giving him some much loved exercise running up and down chasing his ball. She is extremely good with Doodles and the two make a good duo.

Chapter 9

THE UNEXPECTED BENEFITS OF DOODLES' PRESENCE

THE EFFECTS OF DOODLES' UNCONDITIONAL LOVE

One of the delightful aspects of having a puppy in school has been watching the way the children and young people have grown to love him. They are extremely eager to see him in the morning and they cannot wait to alight from their school transport so that they can say hello to him. Our children are always happy to come to school but with the addition of Doodles many of them are chomping at the bit to get into school. They have also grown in confidence. Puppies and dogs love unconditionally. As adults we are aware that this is the case but for our children this has been something they have learned. The dog will always adore them and it doesn't matter if they are tired, grumpy or upset, the dog will always be there for them. Being around Doodles has taught some of them that they will always have someone who will listen to them. This may stop them taking their emotions out on other children. I have actually seen this in action. Some of our older children talk to Doodles and share their secrets and frustrations with him and he of course is non-judgemental. Having expressed their emotions without fear of being in trouble they are then able to carry on with their day in a much better frame of mind.

COOPERATIVE PLAY

Another unexpected benefit of having Doodles has been watching the way the children take turns and organise themselves to play with him. Written into the school policy is the fact that there will always be a responsible adult with Doodles when he is with the children. At break and lunchtime there is no shortage of children wanting to exercise him. I try to take it class by class so that I can see how the children are interacting with him. From my vantage point on the side lines I can see that there is usually one self-appointed leader who takes charge of the proceedings. I don't interfere as this is an excellent way for children to learn those social skills of turn taking, sharing and operating as a team. In Diamond Class we have a group of boys who are able to throw the ball for him as though they are throwing a cricket ball. The dog has to run for quite some distance to retrieve it. The children have swiftly become aware that Doodles has a favourite of the two balls that he plays with. He keeps one ball in his mouth and they throw the other one. In this way Doodles is exposed to lots of exercise and so are the children. The leader keeps a check in his own head of who has had a turn to throw and whose turn it is to run with the dog and directs the action. Strangely, there are no arguments from the children; they are happy to be led in this way. Also within that class there is a girl who is in a powered wheelchair. She has a tiny voice and struggles to be heard. I never need to ask the other children to let her have a turn, they have become so adept at turn taking that they include her in their game. The dynamics of this class are such that there are a number of quite fiery characters within it. It is very pleasing to see that they can organise themselves in such a manner when it suits their purpose.

Key Stage 5 operates in a similar manner without realising it. They also have a self-appointed ring leader who even goes so far as to dictate where everyone will stand when they are playing with Doodles. She organises them like a sergeant major might organise her troops. The young people are ordered to 'play' with Doodles in a certain way. For the most part this works well. However, occasionally there is a little dissent in the team and some of the boys decide that they will buck the system. Again, I am on hand if needed but often when the boys simply walk away the girl realises she has gone too far and backs down a little. This is a big learning curve for her and helps her to realise that she cannot always have everything exactly the way she wants it. This is a life skill and a lesson that everyone needs to learn.

TAKING RESPONSIBILITY

Due to the children exercising the puppy we are now seeing an increase in the level of responsibility shown by them. As our school is a special school many of our children are used to having everything done for them throughout their lives. Their every need is catered for because quite often it is difficult to allow them a level of independence when it is quite possible that by doing so they may be hurt or harmed. Now they have a real live animal that needs their care and attention. After exercising him they take it in turns to accompany myself and Doodles back to my office. They have all adapted their own routines of making him have a drink in order to cool him down and stop him panting and they also remove his lead for him. They quickly worked out that he will chew his lead if left to his own devices so they have decided on a special high place where it will be safe from his teeth. Next up is treat time. If they deem he has been good while playing with them he is allowed a few treats. Each of the children give him two treats; those are the rules made by the accompanying children. By doing all of this they have taken responsibility for ensuring he is fed and watered but not given so much food that he will not want a meal later in the day.

DEVELOPING EMPATHY

This caring side that the children are now developing is progressing very well. If the weather is inclement they don't forget about him. They still come and ask if they can take him for a quick walk. They care so much that even if he can't play out with them they know that he will need a toilet break. This is teaching our children empathy. Through thinking about Doodles they are considering the needs of others. Is he hungry? Is he tired? Does he need to go to sleep? These are all things that they have never considered before and they are now transferring those caring and thoughtful skills to the children in their class.

DOODLES JOINING IN

One of the things the children and young people have said they love most about having Doodles around is that he's always willing to join in. Whatever the occasion Doodles will be there with enthusiasm, even if it's a dressing up day. One good example of this was when a local charity held a 'Wear a hat day' to raise awareness for young carers. Doodles was happy to pose in a hat to encourage everyone else to do the same. He didn't wear it for very long before deciding it had to be removed but he amused the children by wearing it. He posed beautifully in the corridor with our headteacher Rosie who was wearing a very posh hat and the duo looked like they were off to attend a royal garden party. Doodles was also willing to wear a beautiful Santa hat at Christmas time. Again, the hat wasn't in situ for an extended period before he decided to remove it and he subsequently chewed the elastic to ensure he couldn't wear it again. All these little antics simply endeared him more to the children and staff.

COLLECTIVE RESPONSIBILITY

Another benefit of having Doodles in school is seeing the development of collective ownership of a school pet. As I have been writing blog posts about the successes Doodles is having in school we have had several enquiries from teachers and teaching assistants (TAs) in other schools who have read them and have expressed an interest in coming and observing him in action. I try my best to accommodate these requests as we would like other schools to experience the kind of successes we are having. When the visitor arrives I generally have a child or young person with me to explain the role of the dog. It is interesting to listen to them as they tell the visitors how they have been involved in his training, how they exercise him and the different jobs he does in all the classes. The children and young people are quite rightly very proud of their input to Doodles' experiences in school. More than that they become very animated when describing how they play with Doodles and they take turns to speak to our guest. Once again I am able to witness how their social skills are improving along with their turn taking and also their ability to converse with strangers. One of our physiotherapists overheard the older children discussing the pup with a visiting teacher and she told me that she heard the group of children very proudly say, 'He is our dog and we have trained him and we walk him.' That kind of collective ownership should be encouraged as it brings along with it a shared and collective responsibility.

Recently Doodles and I were showing a visitor around the school and we came across a little girl who was walking in her walking frame. For some of our children with extreme physical challenges this may be an uncomfortable or even a painful experience. The physiotherapist and the support assistants use any means at their disposal to encourage the children to walk as far as they can. That particular day Doodles was in the right place at the right time. I gave his lead to the young girl and hey presto she had something else to concentrate on; she was taking Doodles for a walk. Doodles was very gentle with her and instinctively knew that he had to walk slowly and calmly. The girl was very pleased and proud of herself and was beaming from ear to ear. Just at that moment Kayla and Grace from Key Stage 5 emerged from a classroom and saw the dog. Usually when they spot Doodles they immediately fall down on their hands and knees to play with him and fuss him. Both girls took in the situation at a glance and completely ignored Doodles and continued on their way. I was very proud of the girls because of the mature way in which they behaved. I awarded them a Class Dojo each which is the school's reward system. Dojos are highly sought after as the pupil with the most Dojos receives an award at the end of the week so the girls knew they had done something very special. As I returned to my office I saw the headteacher and relayed to her what had happened with the girls and how proud I was. Rosie promptly went to see them and awarded them a Dojo each. Headteacher's Dojos are worth double so they are highly sought after and the girls were pleased with this extra reinforcement of their behaviour.

STAFF SPOILING DOODLES

An unexpected aspect of having Doodles in school has been watching the way the staff have behaved when presented with a school pet. Some have carried on their daily work and apart from saying hello to him they haven't been too affected by his presence. Then there are others who have truly spoilt him. For example, one afternoon I was in a Governors' meeting and it was a very wet day, the rain was bouncing off the floor. My meeting was scheduled to last for a couple of hours but I knew he was due his walk with Andrea so he would be fine on his own after that. On returning from his walk I am told that Andrea dried him off with his own towel and then took him into the school office rather than leave him on his own. Doodles is in his element in that office; it is full of his favourite people and he's even allowed to help open cardboard boxes from time to time. He also has his own toy drawer in there provided by Bridget. After a while Bridget decided to take Doodles for a little jaunt to the staff room with her. Everyone who was on their lunch break patted him and stroked him and he was encouraged up on to the staff chairs and generally spoilt. He had his eye on a flapjack in the hands of a staff member and was about to make a leap for it when he was spotted and removed from what was almost a crime scene. When I returned from my meeting Doodles was back in his crate in my office all snuggled up in his blanket. It was the next day before anyone told me how much he had enjoyed his afternoon without me.

There seems to be quite a common theme with Doodles and the rain. The young pup doesn't have much of an aversion to going out in the rain but the staff seem to think that he will not like it or will come to some harm from going for a walk in the rain. One rainy Thursday morning I had been out with Doodles for a short walk and all was well. I had decided that he could join me in the next lesson which was a speaking and listening group for Key Stage 3. Doodles would encourage them to speak and he is a wonderful subject to discuss. I left him in class with the children and Jill, the Level 4 Nursery Nurse who takes charge if the teacher has to pop out, while I went off to get my resources. When I returned there was no sign of Jill, the class or Doodles. I searched the school as I knew they would be inside somewhere as it was very wet outside. After some time I located them in the cookery room. The entire class had a cup of hot chocolate each and the young puppy was fast asleep on Jill's knee having been blow dried so that he wouldn't be cold from the rain. There were no complaints from Doodles, he loves being spoilt by the staff.

On one occasion the weather was extremely hot. We have a cooling system in school which can generally cope with the extremes of temperature, after all hot weather in this country doesn't usually last long enough to pose too much of a problem. On this day Doodles had been playing with the children, running up and down and chasing a ball. He was very hot and bothered and seemed unable to find any cool relief inside the school. I took him into the school office thinking it might be cooler in there but it wasn't. We found a solution in there though as Claudia our school receptionist took pity on the pup and gave him a fan. Back we went to my office and installed the fan facing towards Doodles' crate. He went into his crate for his afternoon nap and fell asleep with the breeze of the office fan cooling him down beautifully. Anyone who passed him that day commented on what a spoilt pup he was!

— Chapter 10 —

DOODLES IN CLASS

DIAMOND CLASS

Alongside Doodles' success with individual children some classes have made exceptional use of his presence. One of those is Diamond Class and they have really taken him to their heart. Diamond Class is fortunate enough to have a rather talented and creative qualified Level 4 TA, Mrs Todd. Twice during the school year, once in the autumn term and once in the summer term, we collapse the school timetable, abandon the lessons in their usual format and teach all subjects through 'enterprise'. Each class picks their own theme and puts much effort into researching their idea. They find out the cost of producing their items and take a trip out on the school minibus to purchase the things they need. They then use their computing skills to produce advertising posters and finally they sell their goods to visitors and staff. This is the brainchild of one of our assistant heads and is an innovative way to teach real-life skills and the children learn in an exciting way. Furthermore, they are allowed to keep any profits they make so it is in their own interest to make the venture as successful as possible.

Diamond Class, under the guidance of Mrs Todd, chose to make 'Doodles endorsed' doggy treat jars. What a genius idea! They sourced puppy biscuits from the cheapest supplier, purchased them on a trip out and used mathematical skills to weigh them into separate jars. They produced two different sized jars competitively priced at 50p and £1. In order to make their doggy jars look truly professional they came and borrowed Doodles and managed to make him pose for a picture to endorse their jars. They learned new skills of how to download his picture onto the computer, edit it and then create enough prints to adorn their jars. Doodles looked very smart and very proud advertising Diamond Class products and the children sold many 'Doodles endorsed' treat jars to create a tidy profit for themselves.

This was an incredibly sensible idea as the children were able to work with Doodles and the puppy had to be sensible enough to be trusted around the children and the delicious doggy treats.

The ever creative Mrs Todd had another fantastic idea up her sleeve regarding enterprise education. The children and young people are aware that sometimes they have to become involved in social enterprise. This involves encouraging the children to think about social problems and how they as a small business can help. For example, there is a horse rescue and welfare organisation close to our school in Blackpool. It is famous for rescuing and rehoming horses. Mrs Todd discussed the horses with the children. They talked about how some of them had been abandoned and malnourished or poorly treated. They discussed all the money that was required in charitable donations to keep the horses alive, fed, groomed and exercised. The children agreed to donate some of their earnings towards adopting a horse. As the conversation continued it became apparent that the children had no idea how to feed a horse, how to groom it or even how to exercise it. They were one very giddy and excited class when a trip to see their horse, Magpie, was announced. Diamond Class soon found out that the best way to learn is by 'hands on' experience. This is where Doodles came into his own.

Prior to meeting Magpie the class were taught that they had to be calm and quiet around the horse or they might scare him or make him over-excited in which case he might bolt. This of course is how they are supposed to be when Doodles is around. What a fantastic opportunity to learn how to act around animals. They were also taught how to feed the horse by feeding Doodles. At first they were a little reluctant to do this as they thought he might bite them. Up stepped one brave young boy; he held the treats on the flat of his hand, just as you would with a horse, and he fed Doodles. Once he had done it successfully almost all the class wanted to have a try. There were no complaints from Doodles; he's always willing to eat treats. There was still a problem with regards to feeding Magpie that Doodles was able to help out with. Horses have to be fed a certain amount depending on their weight. This is of course exactly how you decide how much to feed a dog. How much does Magpie weigh? How do you weigh a horse? How much does Doodles weigh? How do you weigh a dog? These were questions that Diamond Class had to find answers to. We discovered that weighing a horse is not the same as weighing a dog. We were able to weigh Doodles by first weighing a child, noting the weight and then sitting Doodles on the child's knee. The children decided this wouldn't be practical for weighing a horse and came up with some rather clever alternative engineering-type ideas. One young boy in Year 5, Jay, thought it would be a good idea to have an industrial size set of scales large enough for the horse just to step on to. There would need to be a small ramp for the horse to walk up and it would need to be enclosed in railings so that the horse knew to stand still and also so that it would feel safe and secure. We spent an entire lesson researching how to weigh a horse and Jay was spot on! He was very proud of himself and Mrs Todd and I were very impressed with the class's thinking and problem-solving skills.

Another class trip was planned to visit Magpie and we knew that this time the horse would be well enough for the children to gently groom him. Here was another learning opportunity for Diamond Class. They all took turns to gently brush Doodles and learned how to avoid his eyes and his mouth area. They had learned so much about how to care for animals simply from having the puppy in school. They have also learnt to share and take turns. This is a lesson all children need to learn but this class was struggling with the concept of sharing. They had all joined our school from nearby mainstream schools and were used to having things their own way. Sharing was a big problem for them but it was made easier by them taking turns to play with, feed and groom the dog.

There seems to be no end to the creative use of Doodles from Mrs Todd. Diamond Class' topic for the autumn term was the Second World War. Mrs Todd created a bomb shelter in the classroom with blankets and toys from the 1940s. As we approached Christmas she had the class make traditional paper advent calendars. The children had to write something special to themselves behind every window. Each history lesson when Doodles and I went into the class we joined the children in the bomb shelter, listened to the radio as they would have done during the Second World War and took turns listening to what was behind all the calendar windows. This is a fantastic way to learn by simulating actually being alive during the war. This provided lots of opportunities for replicating family life in the bomb shelter, including taking your dog with you and ensuring that as part of the family he and everyone else was safe.

This section cannot be completed without discussing Casey, a boy in Year 7. Casey joined us at the start of this academic year and due to his learning difficulties he often finds conforming to rules something of a struggle. He is one of the loveliest boys you could wish to meet and he tries so hard to be good but can't always manage it. Casey loves Doodles. School life is now very simple for this boy. He will do anything to take Doodles for a walk around school or to throw the ball for him outside. He is very gentle and caring with the young dog and has really taken to him. His whole topic of conversation centres around Doodles and he is happiest when he is leading his class and holding the dog's lead. Doodles is good for Casey as he is sometimes used as a reward to help Casey do something he isn't too keen on. This is not bribery; it's all about using your best resources to encourage the best behaviour. As Casey is very successful when the dog is around he is in receipt of more certificates and Class Dojos which leads to increased self-esteem. Everyone's a winner in this scenario.

A recent addition to Casey's education is a book which he fondly calls his 'Doodles Book'. Sometimes Casey is not always on his best behaviour and he can let himself down. His emotions sometimes get the better of him and he finds conforming to the rules of the classroom something of a challenge. The ever resourceful Mrs Todd has devised a book whereby Casey collects stars for work done well, staying on task or simply being kind and sharing and he sticks his stars into his Doodles book. His book is covered in pictures of Doodles and he enjoys sticking in his stars. When he has reached the required number of stars he is allowed to come and spend time with Doodles. What a fabulous incentive! Suddenly Casey's behaviour is not such an issue.

RECTANGLE CLASS

One day Doodles and I were on our morning walk around the corridors just meeting and greeting the children and stopping for a quick chat with them if time allowed. We went past Rectangle classroom door and saw all the children sitting in a line. Doodles and I stepped inside to enquire what was happening. Miss Baines the class teacher was conducting a lesson on road safety. She had constructed a makeshift road compete with zebra crossing and traffic beacons. The children were learning their Highway Code and at the very least they were all learning to look right and left before stepping out onto the road.

Much to the delight of the children, Miss Baines decided that Doodles would be a good role model. We had to walk up to the road and Doodles had to sit at the kerbside like you would at the busy main road. We had to look both ways and keep looking and listening as we walked sensibly across the road. The children then took turns to practise crossing the road and enjoyed being in charge of the pup as they did so. Their interest in the lesson was heightened with the addition of the dog. Lots of giggling ensued but a very serious lesson was also delivered.

Miss Baines's Rectangle Class was in charge of assembly one Friday afternoon in February and the topic was Chinese New Year. The class had worked hard making animal masks to wear to show the animals that had symbolised many new years in the Chinese custom. 2018 is of course the year of the dog and Doodles was to have a guest 'walk on' part in their assembly. Miss Baines and I had briefly discussed that Doodles might put in an appearance and simply walk across the stage after the children had done their performance. We hadn't told the children and it was just as well because it didn't happen. I took him into the hall and we sat at the back with some of the staff, away from the children as we didn't want to disturb anyone or upstage the assembly for the young children. Doodles decided that the floor wasn't good enough for him and he jumped onto a staff member's knee. I removed him and sat him back on the floor and he promptly voiced his disapproval with a piercing bark! All eyes were now on Doodles rather than on the assembly performers and Doodles was insistent on sitting on the knee of the member of staff. There was nothing for it; I had to remove him as he was causing a disturbance and spoiling the children's hard work. We left the hall and we missed the assembly that Doodles was supposed to be in. Doodles had some maturing to do before he could participate in an assembly!

PENTAGON CLASS

Pentagon Class are predominantly Key Stage 3 and are therefore over 13 years of age and think they are incredibly grown up. However, they aren't too old to appreciate a puppy. In particular there is a small group of girls in that class who absolutely adore Doodles. Whenever I go to teach in their class it is always part of the deal that I will finish a few minutes before the end of the lesson and they will accompany me to fetch Doodles so that they can have some puppy time. They take him outside on the grass in all weathers and throw the ball backwards and forwards, backwards and forwards many times. For Doodles this is of course just wonderful and, in that moment, these young girls are his best friends. Once again, it's a bonus to have the teenage girls outside taking part in some exercise and having some fresh air. This is obviously a far healthier option than being inside watching YouTube clips. Exercising Doodles has become such a thing between the children and young people that we have had to design some dog-walking certificates. Each week during the school's achievement assembly one or two specially designed certificates are given out to the best dog walkers. These are highly sought after, especially between Pentagon and Diamond Class and if I forget to give them out I find myself in trouble with the children. This was seen most recently after the assembly one Friday when I was approached by a rather glum-looking Jenna in Pentagon Class. She wanted to know if Doodles had forgotten to give out any certificates that week or would she be receiving one. This was a fair enough question as to my great shame I had forgotten to write Doodles' certificates and needed a nudge. I corrected the situation on Monday and Jenna had a smile on her face once again.

SQUARE CLASS

Kalvin is a young man who is not always 'school ready' and he is a valued member of Square Class. Their teacher is Miss Altham and she is the joint PE leader for the whole school. As such she spends a great deal of time delivering PE lessons to different classes. By coincidence PE is one of Doodles' favourite lessons. There are always children running around and balls to be chased. There is lots of shouting and giggling and Doodles loves the excitement and I have to do my best to prevent him from barking and causing mayhem. One day I happened upon a Boccia lesson taking place in the school hall. Many of our children have physical challenges but thanks to our talented staff the game has been adapted and made fully inclusive for all our children. They were having a very exciting game and everyone was taking part except Kalvin who wasn't particularly keen on the various noises. For our visually impaired children there are Boccia balls with bells attached to them. Other balls are made to land with a heavy thump so that everyone knows where they are and there are whistles and clapping all occurring simultaneously. For a young man on the autism spectrum this amounts to sensory overload. Miss Altham produced some heavy duty ear defenders for Kalvin and he had some time out away from the lesson with Doodles to help him get over his anxiety. When he was calm enough to re-join the lesson he went into one corner of the room with his teaching assistant and the two of them played football with

Doodles. This was a creative idea which meant that our young man still had his exercise; he had calmed down after having cuddles with Doodles and was able to play with the puppy as long as he was wearing his ear defenders. Great result!

Sometimes Kalvin will become upset about things which are completely out of our control. Other times he will be worn down by sensory overload and will become disturbed by his surroundings and will need to take some time out, away from his peers in a quiet area of the school. Having some quiet, chilled-out time, usually safely snuggled safely under his weighted blanket helps him to feel that all is well with the world and enables him to carry on with his day. One thing we have found is that this boy loves Doodles even when he is struggling with sensory overload. He has a few minutes to chill out and as soon as he is ready, when the staff tell me the time is correct, I take Doodles in to see him. Doodles sits as quietly and as calmly as he can possibly be. Kalvin who has previously been quite upset calms almost on sight of the dog. He puts his hand out and Doodles licks it very tenderly. This makes Kalvin giggle and he strokes the dog around his neck. Kalvin is 15 years old and like most boys of that age he is fully grown and the size of an adult. He is so gentle with Doodles and it is lovely to witness the way the pup calms him right down. The first time this happened I was quite worried. Throughout the whole interaction I was concerned that Doodles might make a sudden noise or jump up to get closer to Kalvin and startle him. We have no idea what would have happened if that scenario had occurred but sometimes you just have to put your trust in a situation and take a leap of faith. Doodles seems to know instinctively that Kalvin needs him to be calm and he takes this on board and works his magic on him.

Kalvin and Doodles have developed a very good relationship as time has gone on. Another example of the special bond that has grown between these two was seen when I was in our headteacher's office one afternoon. Doodles was being very silly and very puppy like with Rosie. He had climbed on to her knee and was washing her ears for her. She was too busy laughing to scold him so he was getting clean away with his poor behaviour. Down the corridor came Kalvin with his teaching assistant. He had been out for the day on work experience and had been very successful. The park where he had been helping to clear the paths was now looking good and the staff there were very pleased with his progress. He wanted to tell his headteacher of his success. Kalvin and the TA came down the corridor just as Doodles was being very silly in the head's office, but as soon as he saw Kalvin he jumped down on the floor and sat to wait for Kalvin to stroke him. This was first-class evidence that the young pup knew his job and knew how to behave, he was just having a moment of down time with the headteacher.

The very next day Doodles came into his own in front of a visitor from Edge Hill University. He was visiting me to discuss the trainee teachers that we have at our school. I had made our visitor a cup of tea and we set about our business discussing the education landscape. Doodles was determined to be in on the act and was insistent on jumping up at them. He even barked at one point to try and get their attention. He was being really quite a monkey and I had to put him on his lead and make him sit by my side. Kalvin came down the corridor in search of some quiet time away from the noise of his lesson. After a few minutes his TA knocked on my door and asked if Kalvin could see Doodles. Of course I agreed because he loves Kalvin. To the absolute amazement of the visiting lecturer Doodles lay quietly down on the floor next to Kalvin who had already positioned himself on my floor and allowed Kalvin to run his fingers through his curly hair. A few minutes passed by and then Kalvin felt able to return to his class and continue with his lesson. Doodles had changed his mischievous behaviour and our visitor was very impressed and had witnessed at first hand the success that Doodles is having.

MR WALKER'S CLASSES

Not long after Doodles arrived at Highfurlong we were lucky enough to receive a new student teacher, Jason Walker. Jason arrived at the start of Doodles' second half term, just after the summer holidays when the children had missed the puppy over the long vacation. Doodles fever was at an all-time high. Jason was from Edgehill University and was previously a network manager. He has vast knowledge of ICT and was always destined to be an ICT teacher. Jason realised that Doodles was a great hook for his lessons and used him in ever more creative ways.

The first task the young pup was used in was to teach the young people of Key Stage 5 how to design and make their own Christmas cards. Jason was teaching them just how creative they could be with a little imagination. He taught them how to conduct a Google search to find a picture of Doodles on our own school website using an expression search. This in itself is not an easy task for children who have learning challenges. He then showed them a Christmas card decorated with the usual Christmas images such as festive bells and robins. He then used Doodles' image to change the card by adding him as an overlay. The children really bought into the idea and created their own Christmas cards, some featuring Doodles and some merely using the technique they had learned using the dog's picture. This was an inspirational lesson to be involved in and it was a pleasure to see the young people so excited to learn.

Another time Jason used Doodles in his teaching was during a computer coding lesson. The children were given some code similar to the code that was previously used by Roamer, the educational robot. They were given a worksheet to assess their problem solving and computational thinking where they were given some guidance that Doodles was stuck on the starting box and needed their help to get to the exit by crossing through the correct boxes. They were taught to use these algorithms to support in use of OSMO coding and Scratch Junior. They had two puzzles where they had three algorithm answers, two of which were correct. Doodles was used as the character 'sprite' on the starting line and the children had to recognise the patterns to move Doodles along to the finishing line. By using Doodles in this way Jason was assessing them on pattern recognition and computational thinking/problem solving. All the children were keen to have a go and to move Doodles along the line. They all managed to get the answer correct as they were so keen to help Doodles. Through this creative use of the puppy the young people stayed on task throughout the lesson and enjoyed their ICT.

Functional skills maths for Key Stage 5 was the next set of lessons utilised by Jason to capture the interest of the children using Doodles. He took the well-known game of Monopoly, simplified it and adapted it for our students. Much to the amusement of the children he created some Doodles' Dollars. The children were then able to use these to make addition or subtraction calculations based on buying properties or for paying rent to the property owner just as you did in the original game. This was an exceptionally clever idea as the children had no idea they were actually learning any skills. They all thought they were playing a new game of Monopoly.

Jason had a never-ending supply of ideas in which he could use the dog to capture the children's imagination and interest. He created a jigsaw for each child using Doodles' face. The purpose of the jigsaw was to demonstrate that when files are transferred over the network they are broken down into little blocks called 'packets' that are a bit like a jigsaw piece. These bits are split by one computer and then transferred 'super fast' across the network and put together by the other computer. Jason even managed to differentiate the lesson by scaffolding the activity by adding numbers on the back of each jigsaw piece in the same way a packet will have information of how to assemble the blocks. The children would then have a board the same size with the corresponding piece number on. There was also a very slight randomisation of number position to add some challenge for the more able. This involved a switch every four numbers or so. The children loved the lesson and learned a great deal about networking through clever planning and use of the puppy, which was backed by formative assessment.

I could give many examples of the way Jason cleverly used Doodles in his lessons but I will briefly add one more. He planned to teach the young people in Key Stage 5 how to create a poster of their own choosing. Of course he needed a subject to interest them and to demonstrate the skills he was teaching them. What better subject than our ever-willing school dog! He was also going to demonstrate how to be creative when adding pictures to the poster and how to add text that stands out. The children were full of ideas, inspired by the use of the dog, and the end result was that Doodles would be the star in a pantomime and the price, date and venue were all added as extras to the poster. This was excellent planning from the trainee teacher including high expectations of all the young people and of course they rose to the challenge and produced posters of a high standard. Well done that teacher!

MR BIRTLES

Mr Birtles is one of our super-talented middle leaders here at Highfurlong School. He is also the leader of ICT/ Computing and as such he has a keen interest in new and emerging technology. Our school has a digital portfolio for each of our students but Mr Birtles felt that it would benefit from an update as we have had the same one for a number of years. With this in mind he decided to introduce Seesaw as a whole school digital portfolio. As a school we had previously been using the app to allow the children and young people to create posts and share them with their family and friends. It is a good way to introduce the children to social media in a safe and secure manner. They can create their content, post it online and invite their families and friends to comment. They can also reflect on what they have written and correct their own work. In this way parents and siblings are invited to collaborate with school and share in their child's learning. As with all social media and new technology there has to be some ground rules for everyone to follow. Rather cleverly, Mr Birtles decided to use Doodles to introduce and enforce the rules for Seesaw. He explained that Doodles is something that all the children can relate to and if Doodles is 'watching' them it should help to keep those few who might not quite follow the rules on board because it gives the rules a persona. I think Mr Birtles is right; here are 'Doodles' Golden Rules for Seesaw'.

Doodles' Golden rules for Seesaw

Make sure your posts are sensible and are not rude, we don't want to offend anyone.

Only post pictures and videos of people if they allow you to.

If you post a picture or video you <u>must</u> write a caption to tell people what you've posted.

Don't let anyone outside school use your class login.

Only choose your <u>own name</u> when you make a post.

The app is very user friendly and the children are loving being able to post things online at home or when they are out and about at the weekend and their teachers are able to comment instantly. They are also enjoying the fact that Doodles is ever present; he is always keeping an eye on their activities and seeing how they are spending their time away from school.

MISS PAREKH

This year we have been joined by Miss Parekh who is completing a PGCE in education. She is currently teaching in Key Stage 4 and is doing a grand job of using the interests of the young people in her lessons. Just recently I was completing a lesson observation for her as part of her ITT course and was more than happy to see her use Doodles in her lesson. The lesson was an English grammar lesson and the youngsters were working on nouns and adjectives. What finer opportunity to use our very own Doodles. Of course their interest was piqued immediately when Miss Parekh asked them for adjectives to describe Doodles. They came up with a long list of words such as cute, fluffy, handsome, pretty and furry to name a few. They went on to have a discussion around things belonging to Doodles and came up with a further list of doggy related items and adjectives. During the whole of this lesson the young people were involved in turn taking, spelling the adjectives, discussing their interests in details and all while having fun. The young student teacher had planned an interesting lesson for them harnessing something very close to their hearts. I was particularly proud of Miss Parekh because she is absolutely terrified of dogs. She cannot be anywhere near Doodles unless he is on his lead and can't get close to her. Since joining us in September her fear has decreased somewhat. At first she struggled to be in the room with him, such was the strength of her fear. Six months down the line she can now be within a metre of him as long as he is on his lead. I don't think Miss Parekh will ever overcome her fear but I like to think it is slightly more manageable for her thanks to her being around Doodles.

CIRCLE CLASS

Circle Class is a Key Stage 2 class consisting of children with a variety of physical and sensory challenges and also ASC and ADHD. There are 11 children in total in the class, six boys and five girls. One of the boys, Levi, has sensory processing issues, is on the autism spectrum and also has ADHD. Levi struggles to sit still for more than a few minutes and his class teacher, Mrs Short, has introduced some sensory breaks as part of a sensory diet for him to help him deal with his sensory overload with the idea that he will then return to class and be able to stay on task for a little longer. Quite often when Levi is outside with a TA running off some of his energy I am also outside with some children who are playing with Doodles. At first Levi was less than interested in the pup and paid him no attention at all. Then, as time went on he became a little braver and approached Doodles and pulled his tail. Oops! He did this several times before his class teacher explained to him that his behaviour wasn't acceptable and he then reverted to ignoring the puppy. A few months further down the line Mrs Short's class began to utilise the dog more and more. They had a new boy in their class and he, like Levi, was on the autism spectrum and had ADHD and sensory processing issues. The boys were good company for each other. They didn't actually play together due to the challenges they faced but they could share the same activities, share staff and play alongside each other. Both boys struggle with attention span and staying in one place. They can manage to stay on task for around ten minutes if the lesson is highly structured with 'now and next' boards and the use of timers and incentives to keep them on track. A sensory diet is vital for both boys throughout the day: a series of physical activities that may be performed at certain times and at set intervals throughout the day. It is personalised and planned especially for the boys to help them to remain calm and focused when they are in class. Mrs Short spotted an opportunity for Doodles to help out with this one and for his part Doodles was more than happy to do so.

During the morning both boys go together with a TA and bounce a giant ball around in the school hall or they visit the sensory room and have the opportunity to chase each around and play with the PE equipment. Just before lunchtime they go outside with a TA and this is where Doodles comes into his own. The boys and Doodles all run around outside together chasing each other and playing tig. Sometimes Levi goes outside on his own as he faces a real battle with his ADHD and needs extra sensory breaks. One afternoon in late January I was outside with Doodles and a couple of children who were taking turns to exercise him when Levi approached us. Levi has some communication challenges but he did manage to tell me that he wanted to hold Doodles. This was the first time Levi had expressed a desire to be so close to the dog and to be honest initially I was rather taken back. Levi's contact with Doodles had been to ignore him. He had never expressed a desire to be close to the dog so this new development was quite a shock. I gave him the lead and hung on to the slack part of it myself to keep some control of the situation as I had no idea what Levi's intentions were. Levi removed my hand and put himself in sole charge of Doodles. This was truly amazing progress and such an achievement to see the boy caring for the dog. We walked along together all three of us and I thought that Levi wanted to bring Doodles back to my office with me. The children all want to do that and it is considered a treat to be allowed to walk the dog around school. No, that wasn't his intention at all. He took the dog straight over to the playground and put himself and Doodles on the equipment. That made me chuckle out loud. This was brilliant progress, from ignoring him to becoming his friend and sharing the playground equipment in a short space of time. Well done Levi!

On another occasion the other young boy in Circle Class who battles ASC and ADHD wasn't quite school ready one morning and it was decided that he would be better having a little quiet time away from the classroom environment until he felt able to join his class mates and be calm enough to learn. Next to my office we have a lovely little room which is especially designed for children who want some peace and quiet. It works well as it is very soothing and the child and TA can visit the room and talk about any subject they wish to or they can read a book together and help the child to be in the right frame of mind for learning. So the young boy went in with his TA and had a good chill-out session. After a while he indicated that he wanted to see Doodles. His wish was granted and we took Doodles next door to see if he could help the young boy. Next thing we noticed was that the boy was attempting to play tig with Doodles as this was what he had done outside with the pup and had enjoyed it. This was a very sweet moment as the boy attempted to prepare himself for being ready to learn and subsequently the pair went outside to play for a few minutes. Before very long he was in class with his peers and Doodles had a well-earned break.

DOODLES' BIRTHDAY

Within the last week of writing this book Doodles has had his first birthday. He must be the most loved, the most cuddled and the most kissed dog in the world. Leading up to his birthday the children were constantly asking what Doodles would be having for his birthday. Would he be getting presents from everyone, would he be having special treats, what was going to happen? This was something I had never considered before; the children seemed to think that he would have a birthday and celebrate it in a similar way to the way children celebrate theirs. I gently explained to the younger ones that we don't do parties, cakes and cards for dogs, only humans. Some of them weren't happy with this information and decided that it simply wasn't good enough. Diamond Class set about making him his very own birthday card. It had his picture on it, a cake and some candles. When it was time for me to teach in their class I took Doodles with me and the children all sang happy birthday to a rather bemused Doodles. He had no idea what all this extra attention as about but he was lapping it up. The class had wrapped up some doggy treats for him and he was very happy to tear off the paper much to the delight of the children. I had anticipated that I wouldn't be able to ignore this very special birthday altogether, not unless I wanted to upset several children so I had brought in some bite-sized cakes for all the children in school. Once Diamond Class had finished their birthday celebrations I sent them off with a TA and the birthday dog to deliver cakes to everyone in school. The children thoroughly enjoyed Doodles' birthday and they learned to think about others from experiencing his celebrations in school. Some of them were lucky enough to be able to visit all the classes and share out the cakes, which improved their self-confidence and made them feel very generous: another extra bonus from having the dog in school.

DOODLES, THE CHILDREN AND THE SNOW!

In Blackpool our children are snow starved! We haven't seen any snow apart from an odd flurry for many years. I think we have a whole generation of children who have never seen snow. But, this year it snowed! There wasn't a lot but there was enough to cause much excitement around the school. It began snowing during the night and by the time the citizens of Blackpool awoke there was possibly a half a centimetre. Well, this may as well be half a metre for children who aren't used to snow. Of course there wasn't enough for our headteacher to declare a 'snow day' so the children arrived on the transport as usual but that day they were in a state of high excitement. Someone else was equally excited with this new white stuff on the ground and he couldn't wait to go outside with the children. Off we went to Diamond Class and by 9.15 a.m. the children and Doodles were outside having the time of their lives. The young dog was snuffling around in it, chasing around in it and allowing the children to gently throw snowballs at him. To their delight the pup thought he could chase the snowballs and the children thought this was hilarious. Before long we had to go in because one of the young men in Square Class had become a little upset. I had to take Doodles to see if he could help the situation in any way at all. He went up to the young man and allowed him to stroke him. Doodles was absolutely soaking wet from playing in the snow with the children. Kalvin loved the feel of him in this very soggy state and the pair lay down next to each other. Kalvin became calmer as he stroked the pup and Doodles was seizing the opportunity for a rest and a snuggle. Doodles had gone from tearing around at top speed in the snow to quietly lying down and working some calming magic on an upset young man. He loves the chance to be with the children in this way.

— Chapter 11 —

OTHER SCHOOL DOGS

DORA

There are now many dogs working in our schools. Some are in mainstream schools and some are in our special schools. In Blackpool and the surrounding area we are the only special school to have introduced a dog so far. As we have seen he has been hugely successful with our children and they absolutely adore him. My colleague and friend Mary Isherwood is headteacher of Camberwell Park Specialist School in Manchester and she has purchased a relative of Doodles from the same home. Her puppy, Dora, is also going down a treat in her special school and is loved by all. Here are some of the success stories she reported to me.

Right from the very beginning there was lots of interest in Dora from across the school. The children, who have various challenges in life, some medical and some on the autism spectrum, wanted to come over to the head's office and say hello and have a chat with her. As with Doodles, the children were full of questions. They wanted to know how old she is, what she eats, where she sleeps and so on. Every opportunity is a learning opportunity in a school and Dora brought many new questions.

Dora has come into her own in terms of supporting the children who have suffered a crisis of some kind. They have been able to tell her what has upset them or made them angry and as a result of telling all to the dog they have been able to return to their learning much quicker than they otherwise would have. This has been incredibly helpful as children don't always want to talk to a teacher or a teaching assistant. As with Doodles, sometimes just the cuddle from Dora is enough to encourage a child to open up.

Dora has also been into classes to add motivation and interest to topic work. An example of this was when the children were learning about Chinese New Year. One of the classes chose to research the year that Dora was born in, very topical indeed. Dora has also spent some of her time in the library with individual children and small groups of children while she herself was learning to be a reading dog.

Just recently Camberwell Park school had a visit from Ofsted to inspect their school. Dora was mentioned in the 'Outstanding' report as offering affection and comfort to the children. The report goes on to praise her as she sits and listens to children read. The inspector noted that this relaxes the children and helps them to build confidence in their reading skills. High praise indeed from Ofsted, well done Dora!

One thing that both Mary and I have noticed is that the pups have had a visible impact on some of the children who have profound and multiple difficulties. For example, in Manchester one child was observed to unfurl her clenched hands and begin to blink her eyes when Dora was placed on her lap. Similarly, in Highfurlong School we have witnessed a child who is visually impaired showing signs of great delight in the form of big smiles when Doodles snuggles his cold wet nose into her hand. These are the moments when you truly realise what a special impact a puppy is having on children who face such severe challenges on a daily basis.

Mary informs me that Dora has been the stimulus for lots of good literacy work. The children have researched all about her and then completed drawings and pieces of writing which have made up a lovely 'Dora' corridor wall display. The School Council have also had some input into Dora and her existence in school. They have met and agreed some ground rules for working with Dora. This was a very useful discussion as the children learned how to keep Dora and themselves safe.

As with Doodles, Dora has also been a roaring success with the staff. She is the welcome party each morning as staff arrive and is excited to see them all. She makes them smile. Staff at Highfurlong also love to see Doodles in the morning and he in turn is very pleased to see them. Staff at both schools are lifted by the presence of the pup. Dora has been the therapy needed by staff on occasions if they have been upset for any reason. She climbs on their knee for a cuddle and all of the staff love her. Dora is an established part of the Camberwell community.

PIPPA

Recently I have been in discussions with some mainstream colleagues and have discovered that dogs in mainstream schools are having a different experience and are being used in different ways from how Doodles and Dora are being used in our special schools. For example, Baines Endowed Church of England Primary School in Blackpool is proud to have Pippa, an extremely cute nine-month-old cockapoo, in their school with the children. Pippa has been part of Baines' school life since September 2017 and is well loved by all. Her first job of the day is to sit and greet all the children as they come out of assembly each morning. The children enjoy seeing Pippa waiting to greet them and as she is sitting beautifully she is a good role model for them. Children who are displaying good behaviour are allowed to visit Pippa and take her for a walk as a reward for their good behaviour. Immediately we can see that Pippa is being used for positive behaviour management and as a role model. When Pippa visits classrooms she stays quietly at the back of the room and the children take it in turns to go up and stroke her or pet her as a reward for their good behaviour. They also take it in turns to go and read to her. Those who have tried exceptionally hard with their reading may be the ones who are chosen first to read to Pippa. After lunch Pippa is assigned to work with either the behaviour mentor or the learning mentor. She sits in on group or individual sessions with the children, whichever is the most appropriate. Alternatively, Pippa joins in with walk and talk therapy where the children are encouraged to walk with the puppy and to talk to her and tell her what is on their mind. This is an excellent use of the dog as we have already seen with Camberwell Park. Children often open up to a dog when they are reluctant to speak to an adult.

Pippa is also being used to teach the children how to behave around puppies and dogs. This is an important skill as they will encounter many dogs during the course of a day. For example, if Pippa is being a little giddy and excited and too boisterous for the children they have been taught to fold their arms and turn their backs on Pippa and stand very still. The puppy isn't too sure what to make of this tactic and it calms her down beautifully. Presenting the children with Pippa who may be too excited is also an excellent way of calming down children who may also be too excited so this is a two-way learning process. There is also the added bonus that one young boy who is scared of dogs is gradually being desensitised and is slowly showing less fear around the puppy.

Sometimes Pippa is just the incentive needed by some children to encourage them to attend school. For whatever reason, not all children are school ready at the start of the day. If they are aware that they may be able to walk Pippa they are encouraged to come in with a smile on their face. Often she is their first port of call as they come into school; they all want to say hello to her. On the days when she isn't in they want to know where she is and what she is doing. Pippa gives the children something to focus on if they are not too happy. She is well loved by all and is an established part of Baines School.

MARTY AND MURPHY

Marton Primary Academy in Blackpool are the proud owners of Marty and Murphy who are two cockapoos. Marty arrived at Marton in September 2017. He was joined in November by his brother Murphy who had been returned to the breeders due to personal circumstances. The headteacher of Marton saw the impact that Marty was having and agreed to his brother also joining the school.

Both dogs are owned by one of the teachers, and as they are still very young they are still getting used to being in school. They spend most of their time in their owner's classroom so that she is on hand to train them and occasionally they go to other classes as a reward for children who have behaved well or completed exceptional work. Marty attends their celebration assembly each Friday, which is a wonderful incentive for the children as they are allowed to stroke and pet him if they have done well. Both the pups are involved in the school's daily 'mile walk' and they also both go out with the children at playtimes. These two young pups are being used to help keep the children fit and healthy by encouraging them outside at playtime and by doing the daily walk.

Marty has his own Facebook page which is regularly updated and this gives a flavour of what both the dogs are doing in school. One example of Marty's superb work was when a little boy who doesn't like writing did his very best writing and asked if he could take it to show it to Marty. The boy read all his work and Marty wagged his tail in appreciation. The little boy felt very special and was encouraged by this encounter to repeat his writing success again.

Marty and Murphy can boast of many successes in their school. For example, they have helped a Reception child to overcome her fear of school by simply being there to greet her in the morning. Now she is happy and excited to come into school. The pups spend time in the classes that have achieved 100 per cent attendance the previous week. This type of collective class reward is a wonderful use of the dogs. Everyone aims to attend for the whole week and everyone is allowed to share in the prize. Also, the dogs are used as a reward for the children who have become 'reading millionaires'; what a wonderful incentive to improve their reading.

I was told that Marty really came into his own when a six-year-old girl fell over and badly hurt herself. Her elbows and knees were grazed and she was visibly shaken, a little hysterical and very pale. Two members of staff were doing their best to calm her down and were bathing her cuts and bruises when Marty arrived on the scene. The little girl started to stroke him and immediately her smile began to return and within a few minutes she was laughing. The transformation was amazing and all a result of the presence of the puppy.

The brothers are also being used as a kind of restorative practice. They sit with the children who have had an argument so they can talk it through and listen to each other in a calm and civilised manner. They can then come to an agreement about how to end their disagreement. The children are reluctant to continue shouting in front of the dogs as they have been taught not to use raised voices around them.

Marty has also been attending Forest School with the children which he really enjoys. Forest School offers all children the opportunity to achieve and develop their self-esteem through hands-on learning in a forest or nature area. Once Marty is at Forest School he is allowed off his lead and has a completely mad ten minutes running and sniffing everywhere. Once he's explored his new environment he calms down a little and potters around at a more leisurely pace taking in what the children are doing. He watches it all with great interest and the children talk to him and explain to him what they are doing. They have made him rope toys with knots in for him to chew on and to pull with. Through activities such as this the children are learning a great deal about science and the properties of certain materials. This is a very creative use of Marton's school dog.

Lastly, their owner is in the same position as I am of late: no one ever says good morning to her, only to the dogs! The staff visit her for a Marty/Murphy hug if they haven't had a good session and she is largely ignored. I completely understand this and often think I have become invisible since I introduced Doodles to school. It's all in a good cause so we don't mind really.

REBA

Reba belongs to Athena, Educational Diversity Pupil Referral Unit (PRU). The PRU provides education for children who can't attend school for various reasons such as social, emotional or medical challenges. It caters for children from Key Stage 2 right through to Key Stage 4. The staff are dedicated to helping these children return to mainstream school as soon as possible and work very hard to ensure this happens. Reba's owner is a speech and language therapist who knows that communication is at the heart of many problems faced by our children. Reba is now 18 months old and joins lessons regularly. Often she just stays at the back of the room quietly supporting the children as they work. At other times she is allowed to amble around the classroom and the children stroke her as she passes by; they simply take comfort from her presence. I was chatting about Reba's success with their assistant headteacher and she told me that Reba has had unprecedented success with children who are refusing to speak. Selective mutism is a complex anxiety disorder that prevents a child from communicating effectively. Since the introduction of Reba the staff have noticed that the children will converse with the dog. This is a phenomenal breakthrough for the PRU and for Reba. Right from the start we wanted Doodles to be a reading dog. Recently he has undergone some training to enable him to do just that. When he first entered school he was very young and he was unable to sit with the children long enough for them to read to him. He was always tempted to tug at their books. We know from research that children grow in confidence when a non-judgemental animal is sitting beside them. Now that he is older he is able to do this and with a little guidance from myself he is able to sit with a child while they read to him. He looks to the outside world like he's giving the story his full attention and listening intently. The reality is that he has matured enough to sit calmly and he is secure in the knowledge that he will receive a treat after doing so.

POPPY

The last mainstream school I will mention is Revoe Learning Academy, a large primary school with a dog called Poppy. Poppy hit the headlines in the *Blackpool Evening Gazette* recently for the creative way that Revoe are using her charms for the benefit of their children. The idea is that Poppy is used as an incentive for the children to come to school on time. Each child who arrives at school on time for a whole week has their name put into a hat with their teacher choosing one name each Friday afternoon. Poppy goes into assembly carrying a much coveted golden ticket in her mouth and presents it to the winning child to the backdrop of the tune 'Gold' by 1980s pop group Spandau Ballet. The ticket is well worth winning because it gives a variety of prizes. One week the prize was a free pass to the local trampoline park for ten weeks – very definitely worth winning – and all recent prizes have been of similar value.

From looking at the way the dogs are used in mainstream school and comparing it to the way Doodles and Dora are used in our special schools there seems to be a common theme. In the mainstream schools the dogs' main remit seems to involve an emphasis on positive behaviour management. In our special schools there is a definite slant towards the nurturing side of things: the caring and sensory experience. All the dogs are used for academia where appropriate and all used in innovative and creative ways for the good of our children. Hats off to all the clever staff for their endless ideas.

— Chapter 12 —

MISCHIEVOUS DOODLES!

Throughout this book I have emphasised all the successes Doodles has had regarding the care and attention he has lavished on our children and young people. He has been there for them, whatever they have needed, right from the moment he entered school back in June 2017 when he was just an 11-week-old puppy. For all his successes he has also been rather mischievous at times and continues to be something of a minx to this day. For example, Christmas brought its own trials and tribulations for the young pup. He tried very hard to be good but didn't always quite make it. His first challenge was the Christmas trees; as with many schools they were everywhere in Highfurlong. Each class had their own tree and they were all brightly decorated with balloons, tinsel, baubles and presents. All the tree decorations were highly coloured and proved to be just too much of a temptation for Doodles. Whenever we walked past the one in the entrance hall he pulled towards the tree and helped himself to a bauble. Now let me tell you that our little pup was incredibly fast. He would launch himself towards the tree before I had even realised that he had seen it. He always came away triumphant with a beautiful bauble attached to his mouth. The tree lost several baubles that way. Even when I grew wise to his tricks he was still too fast for me and the tree was almost bare after a week. When we ventured into classrooms as part of our daily routine he was by now quite a master at stealing tree decorations and managed to help himself to a few from each class, much to the amusement of the children. One day, we were in the corridor and Doodles was sitting beautifully by my side as though he was the best behaved pup in the world when he spotted a piece of tinsel dangling precariously from the tree, just out of his reach. He bided his time and then made a sudden leap for the tinsel and almost knocked the entire tree over in his determination to have it. After that incident we took to walking along the corridors almost plastered to the wall furthest away from the tree. I had finally learnt my lesson that the young pup wasn't going to stop attacking Christmas trees. Maybe next year!

Christmas presents also posed a real problem for Doodles. He absolutely loved presents. Class teachers had meticulously wrapped up presents for under the tree for the children in their classes. Doodles wasn't above opening them if he wasn't kept on a very short lead. He didn't stop there either; just to add insult to injury he would have the paper off before I noticed he had got the present and would be playing with the toy right in front of the class teacher and the children. Of course the children loved this naughty side of Doodles and actively encouraged him to try and grab a present or some other forbidden object.

Another example of Doodles being rather mischievous was seen when we had more animals in school. Doodles was slowly growing accustomed to seeing Trev the tortoise whenever he went into Circle Class. He continued to pull towards his tank to check if Trev was in there or if he was out having his daily exercise. He would sniff around the whole classroom until he had located the tortoise and then he would stick his nose up close and personal with Trev's face. I always ended up having to beat a hasty retreat with Doodles as I was worried that he would be too boisterous for the tortoise and try and turn him over with his nose. That would not have been well received by Trev's owner, Mrs Short.

Several times a year we have Country Classrooms come and visit us in school. This company offers a unique opportunity to bring a farm into the classroom. Sometimes they bring calves, lambs and ducks and the children learn how to care for them, feed them and all about life on a farm. In February this year the company brought their hatching experience into school. This is a chance for the children to watch the chicks hatch right there in their own classroom. The chicks then visit each classroom for a day so that all children can see them and handle them. One particular day the chicks had arrived in Circle Class just as Doodles and I were en route to pick up some resources from that room. Neither of us had any idea the chicks were there. I strode into the classroom in a purposeful manner as I knew that I was heading to a certain area of the room. Just at that moment, Doodles gave such a sharp tug and lurched backwards so quickly that he almost pulled me over! It's rare that I raise my voice to him, he's a puppy after all and won't understand, but I did raise my voice that time. The naughty pup carried on pulling on his lead so I had to go and investigate what had got him so excited. At that moment in time he didn't know himself what was in the room, all he could see was something moving inside yet another tank. He probably thought it was another Trev. I composed myself and went over and established that the chicks in a gorgeous shade of brown/yellow were shuffling around in their incubator. Mrs Short arrived and we decided to let Doodles have a closer look as long as he didn't frighten the babies. He snuck up to them and stood on his hind legs to have a closer look. He pawed at the tank with his front paws and far from being frightened the baby chicks came forward to investigate the noise. They scrabbled around on top of each other to have a closer look at this giant black animal that was next to their tank peering in. They weren't in the least bit bothered about him and were making quite animated noises. It was an enchanting sight to see all the animals in such close proximity and none of them were worried by the presence of the others. Of course Doodles couldn't contain himself for ever; he had to spoil it by giving a very loud high-pitched bark. However, he was good for quite a few minutes in the presence of the chicks and I was very impressed.

We see Doodles' mischievous side each morning as he wears his dayglo coat and goes outside with our site supervisor to welcome the children and young people into school. This is a lovely welcome for the children, but they have no idea what goes on behind the scenes to create that warm welcome. Doodles puts up a fight every single day about wearing his coat. He has no real objection to wearing it, he just loves playing. It takes Mr Tinkler a handful of doggy treats to pop the coat on the dog. Once he is inside it he goes off happily wagging his tail to do his first job of the day. That's the theory, but it's all in the timing. If he has his coat put on too soon and he has to sit and wait by the door he will lie down and he is clever enough to grab the velcro in his teeth and swiftly remove the coat so the whole saga has to begin again. It takes us a while longer but Mr

Tinkler and I have devised a method of tucking the velcro into the strap that goes around his stomach. To his great frustration there is no way that Doodles can remove his coat if it is put on in that manner. Once the children are safely in school it is time to remove the coat. You can be forgiven for thinking this would make Doodles happy. Not so, now he has the coat on he is keeping it on! Mr Tinkler has perfected the art of removing the coat in one very swift move so that even Doodles is taken by surprise and can't prevent it. There is a look of sheer surprise on the dog's face on a daily basis as the coat is removed and put in a safe place away from his teeth. I'm sure that given time Doodles will work out how to hang onto his coat but for now the site supervisor is winning.

In early March a new teaching student arrived at our school. He has embarked on a PGCE so needs to be up to speed pretty quickly. I had a phone call and an email or two from Richard before he arrived to ensure we were ready for his placement to begin. We almost always have teaching students in school so another one shouldn't be any different. However, Richard is a wheelchair user so we had to ensure that a parking space was reserved and his school pass was available as soon as he arrived. What I hadn't anticipated was Doodles' reaction to Richard. As soon as Doodles saw him he began to bark very loudly. I was annoyed and also embarrassed because this was not a good first impression for the student. I had no idea what was wrong with Doodles and all I could do was remove him from the situation. I took Doodles away and caught up with Richard and explained that Doodles barks at everything he doesn't understand. I told him that he is super friendly and he would be fine with him next time Doodles saw him. I was wrong. Doodles barked again, and again and again! It was very awkward and

I had no idea what was causing it. A few of us brainstormed what might be the problem; it certainly wasn't the wheelchair because we have several young adults in wheelchairs. Maybe it was his tie or his beard, we had no idea but I had to put a stop to the barking. Luckily Richard wasn't in the least bothered and was willing to keep trying to win the pup over. On day 4 of Richard's placement I decided that enough was enough. I took Doodles and some puppy treats and off we went to find Richard. Doodles began his usual barking on sight of Richard. I immediately gave the student some dog treats which he offered to the pup by holding them in the palm of his hand. Doodles was of course silenced by the treats and I was able to give Richard some more for the pup. Like most puppies Doodles will do anything for a tasty treat. Richard was able to use the treats and get closer to the pup and show him that he would be his friend. He stroked and patted him and generally made a fuss of him. We had won that battle, but had we won the war? What would happen tomorrow when Richard and Doodles met in the corridor? That was the question. The next morning Richard and Doodles did indeed meet in the corridor. Doodles ran up to him and stood on his hind legs and threw his front paws on his knees and began licking his hands. This was his friend who fed him treats. Later that same day, Richard came to my office for a meeting. Upon entering the room Doodles jumped on to his knee and proudly sat there as though it was a perfectly normal place for a puppy to sit. He had gone from barking incessantly at him to becoming his best friend. I think the mission had been too successful! I had to forcibly remove him from Richard's knee as we weren't progressing very far with our work. As time continues I may need to look at a strategy for stopping him from jumping on the knees of adults who are in wheelchairs. He will not always be a welcome passenger.

DOODLES AND OUR HEADTEACHER

When I first began exploring the idea of having a school dog on the premises on a regular basis I knew that I needed the permission of our headteacher, Mrs Rosie Sycamore. It is her school and I wasn't sure how she would react to the idea. I knew that I needed her fully on board just in case there was ever a problem. Rosie is all about the children and young people and once she had conducted some research she could see the benefit of having the pup in school. What we hadn't anticipated was that Doodles would be exceptionally mischievous around her. I rather naively hoped he would show her his best side and she would see his potential. Right from the start he adored the boss. When she visited my office she would sit in one of the chairs opposite me while we chatted and up would jump Doodles. He wasn't content with sitting on her knee; as if that wasn't bad enough he would attempt to lick her ears. He was very persistent too and it was quite difficult to have a serious conversation with her while she was being kissed by Doodles. She would pop him down on the floor but Doodles was like a jack in a box and would pop straight back up again. In some ways it was almost as though he was the only one in school who had no respect for her authority. When Rosie and I had completed our conversation she would carry on back to her own room and Doodles would jump straight into her chair. It was as though he was saying 'if it's good enough for her then it's good enough for me'. Slowly but surely he began to claim the headteacher's chair for his own. You can see how that was going to go. When Rosie came into my room he was very pleased to see her but she generally had to physically remove him from her chair and on to the floor whereupon he would jump straight onto her lap and shower her with kisses. She struggled to discipline him because he did show her a lot of love and attention.

On several occasions when we passed Rosie's door Doodles would pull to go in and see her. She always said hello to him and fussed him before she and I had a conversation. Rosie has several well-tended plants dotted around the school, one of them is just inside her doorway and looks beautiful as you enter her office. You don't have to look too closely to see puppy teeth marks in some of the leaves! Goodness knows how he can chew a plant right under our noses but it seems he can.

It is fair to say that Rosie is very soft with Doodles but one day she actually had to become stern with him. I was in another part of the school teaching and Doodles was in his crate in my room enjoying an afternoon nap. There were some workmen around the building and he had no idea who they were. Doodles is not content when he doesn't understand things and he started to bark. I was totally oblivious to this as I was a good distance away. Rosie told me afterwards that she had gone in and told him in a firm voice, 'Quiet Doodles', and he had actually listened to her and stopped barking! This had never worked before and has never worked since. I think he was shocked at the serious headteacher tone to her voice and decided to pay attention just for once. When I returned and he came out of his crate I listened to this tale and watched as Doodles jumped on her knee and began tugging at the scarf around her neck, normality had returned and Doodles was back to his mischievous self.

Over the last few months, since acquiring Doodles, one thing we have discovered is that he doesn't like to be left out of anything. Staff meetings are his favourite thing. Once a week we have a whole school staff briefing which takes place in the staffroom. The first time Doodles attended the meeting it was a total disaster! I said I wouldn't allow him to attend again until he was more mature and more responsive to commands. On that particular Monday morning he jumped up on the chair and refused to move. I tried several times but as the staff meeting is only very short the whole staff were in danger of missing the head's briefing due to Doodles causing a disturbance so I decided to cut my losses and deal with him afterwards. From his vantage point on the chair he could see out of the windows and on to the main road. He set up the loudest bark imaginable until I had no alternative but to remove him from the meeting. I had to apologise to Rosie for his rudeness and I said I wouldn't take him again. I stuck to my word until January this year when I was running late so had no alternative but to take him with me. Surely by now at ten months old he would be able to behave for a quick briefing. I have to admit that he couldn't and he disrupted the whole briefing by jumping on various members of staff and delivering kisses all round. In his defence he was encouraged in this behaviour by some staff who are always eager for puppy cuddles. Once more we left the meeting and one of us was pleased with himself and one of us was a little embarrassed.

As Doodles has matured slightly he has started to listen to commands occasionally. It all depends on the command and if he thinks there might be something in it for him. I have to keep my office door closed when Doodles is in there. This is for two reasons. The first is that some of the children will just pop in and say hello to him and expect to play with him as they pass my door and that isn't appropriate. Doodles' time has to be properly controlled and negotiated with the class teacher. The second reason is that Doodles himself cannot be trusted to stay in my room. If he realises that something exciting might be happening in a different part of the school he will take off in search of some fun. We know this as we witnessed it first hand. Someone had been in to discuss something with me and had left the door slightly ajar. Ever the successful escape artist Doodles seized his opportunity and ran out of the door. My commands of 'wait' resonated down the corridor and fell on deaf ears; the young pup was on a mission. He had smelt the food coming from the school hall and had decided that he needed to investigate and see if there was any for him. He ran at such a pace there was no catching him. He entered the school hall as the children were all eating their lunch. He ran around wagging his tail and saying hello to everyone while a few fit and healthy TAs tried to stop him. He was having the time of his life! To his great credit he didn't help himself to anyone's food and was eventually stopped in his tracks by a teaching assistant. Since that incident I have kept my office door firmly closed and we have practised 'stop' and 'wait' at every opportunity.

DOODLES WANTS HIS OWN WAY

On reflection not all of Doodles' behaviour can be attributed to him being mischievous. Some of it is simply a straight case of him wanting his own way and being rather wilful. An example of this spoilt behaviour is when he sees a certain hat and pair of gloves. Since we have had Doodles Andrea has rarely failed to walk him twice a day. As the weather grew colder she needed a hat and gloves just for exercising the dog. It made sense for her to keep them in my room. Doodles spotted the outdoor wear and when he thought it was time for his walk he started to jump up for the hat and gloves and bark. There was no ignoring the noise he was making and even when I removed them from sight he still continued to demand his walk. The cold weather gear was eventually banished from the room. Not content with that, when Andrea was all dressed for the great outdoors complete with coat with fur hood the pup would jump on her knee and attack her furry hood. On occasions there would actually be a growling noise as though he was trying to worry a small animal. For some reason Doodles had it in his head that Andrea's clothes were for his enjoyment only and there was a daily kerfuffle about this.

A further example of Doodles wanting his own way came to light when he decided that he wanted to sit in the headteacher's chair in my office. He really thinks he is that important! From that elevated, advantageous position he is able to see the children playing outside at break time. Sometimes we go outside and join them, other times I may be busy and cannot spare the time. Doodles, of course, does not understand this and when he sees the children playing outside it is his greatest wish to go and join them. He starts whining very loudly and running around and this eventually builds up into an ear-piercing bark. I'm afraid I have made a rod for my own back with this one because I often give in to him as I am unable to bear the noise. I am quite sure that Doodles knows if he makes too much noise I will eventually give in and take him out to play.

One discovery I have made quite recently has been of great value when Doodles is acting in that way and being boisterous and noisy and refusing to calm down.

It happened quite by chance one Sunday morning when I was at home. I was thinking about Tuesday and the fact that I would be out of school on a course for a good deal of the day. I was mulling over what to do with Doodles when our neighbour knocked on the door and Doodles began leaping around like a three-month-old puppy when they came in. Now that Doodles is 12 months old this type of behaviour, cute as it might be, is becoming inappropriate. He is excellent with the children and his successes have far exceeded our hopes. The children adore him and he is a real positive addition to the school staff. However, his behaviour around adults is another matter altogether.

So, our neighbour came into the house and Doodles' behaviour was absolutely ridiculous! Frank, our neighbour, bent down and held the dog quietly and firmly in a strong hug position. Doodles visibly calmed down before my very eyes. This hug was reminiscent of the deep pressure hugs resulting in proprioceptive feedback that special school staff might give to children. I'm not exaggerating at all when I say that the dog calmed down immediately and what's more he stayed calm! Who knew that adolescent dogs would benefit from deep pressure hugs? I certainly had no idea of this. I asked my fellow educators on Twitter for their thoughts on this and to my great surprise I discovered that many people already knew about this. In fact, there is a whole industry dedicated to producing jackets for calming dogs that are of a nervous disposition. Doodles is far from being in that category but he is in need of calming down when he becomes overexcited. The coats, jacket or vests are produced by ThunderShirt and apply gentle, constant pressure to dogs that need it for various reasons. After this enlightening Twitter discussion I am now considering purchasing one for Doodles. Doodles does not need a ThunderShirt for school as he is generally calm around the children. However, one might be handy for calming him down at home. Some of our children benefit from deep pressure provided by weighted jackets and it helps them to stay calm and in control of their own emotions.

One thing we have discovered with Doodles is that his behaviour is somewhat different at home from at school. At school he does a grand job of looking after the children, cheering them up, teaching them to share and take turns and how to act around pets. He has been very valuable in increasing the family aspect of school life and the children have loved the feeling of collective ownership of a pet. He has added excitement and constructive meaning to academic lessons and his presence has been well received by the children. A completely different story has to be told of his behaviour at home!

In the home Doodles is the most mischievous young dog I have ever come across. Wherever I go Doodles is my constant companion. If I set off to go upstairs Doodles comes with me. He can run up the stairs faster than a cheetah and I cannot stop him. Once upstairs he makes a beeline for the bathroom and emerges at the speed of light with the toilet roll in his mouth. From there the battle is on! Everyone will have seen the famous advertisement on the television where the puppy runs down the stairs with the toilet roll. That pup has nothing on Doodles. He will run downstairs leaving the trail behind him and what is left of the roll is then shredded into millions of tiny pieces. You have never seen such a mess in your life. Initially I tried being stern with him and commanding him to drop it, but he ignores me. I have tried ignoring his behaviour thinking he will grow bored of this game, but he never does. I have tried squirting him with water to shock him into dropping it and still he refuses to release it. The only solution is to keep the bathroom door closed to prevent Doodles from entering in the first place, but how do we know if the bathroom is occupied or not? Some weekends the score for the toilet roll battle is as high as 4-0 to Doodles.

Human clothes are potentially Doodles' favourite thing in the world. If ever something is lost we always search the dog first. His bed has to be checked and all his favourite places must be investigated as he is a master at hiding things. When my hairdresser arrives Doodles is always on hand to help her remove her scarf from her neck. This wouldn't be any problem if she weren't in a standing position at the time. Once she has emerged from her coat and scarf she folds them up and neatly places them on the table. They don't stay there for very long as Doodles will jump onto the table and drag her belongings away to his bed. One day we will remember to put them out of his reach before battle commences.

I could continue for a whole chapter discussing the difference between Doodles' behaviour at home and school. This small taster of the way he behaves at home will suffice. This type of errant behaviour is conventional for young puppies; however, Doodles is old enough to know better now that he is a year old. I sometimes wonder if he is using up all his good behaviour at school and he has to let off steam when he is at home. It's important to remember that he is only having fun at home and there is no real harm being done. If I had to choose I would always opt for him putting in a good performance at school. It is essential that he behaves in an exemplary manner when he is around our children. That aspect is non-negotiable.

— Chapter 13 —

FUTURE PLANS

As Doodles grows and matures we are hoping that his role will expand and he will take on more responsibility. Right at this moment he has enjoyed unparalleled success over and above what we hoped for on the caring, nurturing side of school life. We are now formulating plans for his future in more and more lessons. The first thing we are aiming to do is to train him to be a listening dog. This was one of his original intended roles that hasn't quite yet come to fruition. He listens beautifully to the children when they share their secrets with him but if they have a book in their hand he still sees it as his mission to relieve them of the book.

I have also discussed using Doodles with Mrs Short, our Key Stage 2 leader and also our English/drama/music leader. Mrs Short has identified that she would like to use Doodles in several of her lessons. As the class teacher she thinks he could be very beneficial in maths lessons during the summer term. As in many special schools we leave the capacity topic until the summer term so that the children can learn about water and liquid capacity outside in the fresh air without making the classroom into a paddling pool. Doodles will of course thoroughly enjoy this topic. He will be right there in the centre of the water play and make it so much more fun for the children. He will bring new meaning to the term 'learning through play'. As a young dog he won't mind how much water comes his way; he will love being with the children and helping them to learn. We will of course discourage them from measuring half litres of water out and tipping it over Doodles but I do envisage there being the odd accident.

Doodles can also be used in maths lessons to help the children to develop memory skills. A doggy related version of the popular game 'Kim's Game' will see us using dog accessories to help children develop their memory. For example, Doodles' toys and clothing can be laid out on the table and then covered with a cloth. Children will then try and remember all Doodles' items that are underneath the cloth. They will have an added interest in this game as the items belong to the pup who will of course be trying to take back his belongings.

Doodles will also be able to help the children to master the skill of keeping a tally chart as part of their maths curriculum. Key Stage 1 have plans to take a trip outside of the school grounds and count the number of dogs that pass by our school. Doodles will accompany them as an added bit of fun. On their return they will be able to practise making a tally chart of all the dogs they have seen. This can also be developed to include bar or line graphs as an extra way of showing their data.

Mrs Short, as performing arts leader, is also responsible for the shows the school produces at Christmas and during the last few weeks of the summer term. Highfurlong is a fully inclusive school and every single child and young person takes part in these very popular shows. Some have more help than others in order to allow them to participate but every member of the school is proud of their part in the shows. This seems a very appropriate opportunity for Doodles to take his place alongside the rest of the school community. The themes for the shows chosen by Mrs Short are varied but I fully expect Doodles to have a walk on part as he grows in maturity. The children will enjoy having Doodles as a co-star.

Further plans for Doodles to be included in more of the school day involve some of our anxious children. As we are a special school we like to take our children and young people out on the school minibus to enhance their learning. Sometimes catching a glimpse of the item or building you are learning about is the best way to learn. This is not ideal for all of our pupils as some become very anxious because of the change of routine. Not everyone appreciates swapping the classroom for the minibus and on occasions if not carefully handled this could result in a meltdown for the child. Doodles will come into his own in a situation such as this. He is happy travelling in cars and is used to being fastened in with his own seatbelt for safety reasons. Having Doodles sitting next to an anxious child will help them to overcome their fears. They will be able to think about the dog and stroke him rather than concentrating on their own fears and worries.

One last area that we have plans to use Doodles in concerns Key Stage 5. Just like all other sixth form students our young people are involved in external accreditation. Gaining as many qualifications as possible is their goal and the teaching needs to be very special in order to draw our young people in and keep them on task. We choose all our courses very carefully to ensure that they are as interested as possible in the subjects being studied. At this moment we are looking for a course for external accreditation which will involve caring for small animals. If we can identify one, the young people will learn how to feed, bath, groom, exercise and generally take care of a dog. They will be able to be 'hands on' and learn to give Doodles a bath and they will learn how to brush his fur and keep him tangle free. They will learn to weigh out his dried food and the reasons why he mustn't be over fed. They will learn how much exercise is healthy for an animal of his size and they will be able to take him out for a run on the field. Their maths and literacy skills will improve as a result of undertaking this work. The young people will also learn a valuable life skill as some of them will go on to live independently and may wish to own a pet. Best of all, our youngsters will have fun while they are learning all these skills.

With an eye to the future we would eventually like to start a Facebook page dedicated to Doodles. As a school we have a Facebook page and it is very popular with parents and the wider community. Many people log onto our page in order to follow the activities the children are participating in and to see how much they enjoy their learning. I have seen a Facebook page for a school dog and I think that very soon we will be introducing an account which will follow the adventures of Doodles the school dog. Many of the parents would enjoy this and I have received two requests for this already.

Doodles has been in school with us now for 18 months and since he was 11 weeks old. During the holidays he is a very different young dog and he misses the level of exercise the children and young people give him. When we are out and about taking a walk during the holidays if we see a child in close proximity Doodles will always pull to see if he knows the child. Obviously, he rarely does but as he is a school dog he is more than happy to socialise with any children he comes across. Doodles is regularly checked over by a vet to ensure that he is fit and healthy and emotionally able to be with children. He has had some training with a local qualified Animal Assisted Therapist and he thoroughly enjoyed his sessions. He proved that he is quick to learn and willing to please as he mastered the things he was taught. When he is in school if he shows any reluctance to leave his bed it is written into the policy that he will not leave his safe space. He has never shown such reluctance but we have a contingency plan just in case. Since September we have a new headteacher at the helm. He is a dog lover and truly believes in having dogs in school. He has also turned his office into a safe space for Doodles. He has his own bed in the head's office and treats at the head's discretion. A recent Ofsted inspection brought praise for Doodles as they witnessed first hand the impact he was having with the children.

Doodles has been the most popular member of staff we have introduced in a long while. We hope his success continues unabated and the children continue to thrive and benefit from his presence. The parents have also taken Doodles to their hearts and if he isn't in school they ask after his welfare. If any school is considering the benefits of a school dog we would highly recommend you introduce one as ours has brought much entertainment, joy and educational value.